Crystallization-Study
of
1 and 2 Peter
and Jude

Volume One

Witness Lee

The Holy Word for Morning Revival

Living Stream Ministry

Anaheim, CA • www.lsm.org

First Edition, January 2008.

ISBN 978-0-7363-3617-8

Published by

Living Stream Ministry
2431 W. La Palma Ave., Anaheim, CA 92801 U.S.A.
P. O. Box 2121, Anaheim, CA 92814 U.S.A.

Printed in the United States of America

08 09 10 11 12 13 / 9 8 7 6 5 4 3 2 1

Contents

Preface

1. This book is intended as an aid to believers in developing a daily time of morning revival with the Lord in His word. At the same time, it provides a limited review of the winter training on the "Crystallization-study of 1 & 2 Peter and Jude" held in Anaheim, California, December 24-29, 2007. Through intimate contact with the Lord in His word, the believers can be constituted with life and truth and thereby equipped to prophesy in the meetings of the church unto the building up of the Body of Christ.

2. The entire content of this book is taken from the *Crystallization-study Outlines: 1 & 2 Peter and Jude,* the text and footnotes of the Recovery Version of the Bible, selections from the writings of Witness Lee and Watchman Nee, and *Hymns,* all of which are published by Living Stream Ministry.

3. The book is divided into weeks. One training message is covered per week. Each week presents first the message outline, followed by six daily portions, a hymn, and then some space for writing. The training outline has been divided into days, corresponding to the six daily portions. Each daily portion covers certain points and begins with a section entitled "Morning Nourishment." This section contains selected verses and a short reading that can provide rich spiritual nourishment through intimate fellowship with the Lord. The "Morning Nourishment" is followed by a section entitled "Today's Reading," a longer portion of ministry related to the day's main points. Each day's portion concludes with a short list of references for further reading and some space for the saints to make notes concerning their spiritual inspiration, enlightenment, and enjoyment to serve as a reminder of what they have received of the Lord that day.

4. The space provided at the end of each week is for composing a short prophecy. This prophecy can be composed by considering all of our daily notes, the "harvest" of our inspirations during the week, and preparing a main point

with some sub-points to be spoken in the church meetings for the organic building up of the Body of Christ.

5. Following the last week in this volume, we have provided reading schedules for both the Old and New Testaments in the Recovery Version with footnotes. These schedules are arranged so that one can read through both the Old and New Testaments of the Recovery Version with footnotes in two years.

6. As a practical aid to the saints' feeding on the Word throughout the day, we have provided verse cards at the end of the volume, which correspond to each day's Scripture reading. These may be cut out and carried along as a source of spiritual enlightenment and nourishment in the saints' daily lives.

7. The *Crystallization-study Outlines* were compiled by Living Stream Ministry from the writings of Witness Lee and Watchman Nee. The outlines, footnotes, and references in the Recovery Version of the Bible are by Witness Lee. All of the other references cited in this publication are from the published ministry of Witness Lee and Watchman Nee.

Winter Training

(December 24-29, 2007)

CRYSTALLIZATION-STUDY
OF
1 & 2 PETER AND JUDE

Banners:

In Christ's death
we have been separated from sins, and
in His resurrection we have been enlivened
so that we might live to righteousness
under the government of God.

We must redeem the time to enjoy Christ
as the supreme preciousness of God
so that He can build Himself into us
to make us His spiritual house
and His holy and royal priesthood
for the accomplishment of His heart's desire.

We should be diligent
to pursue the growth and development
of the divine life and divine nature
for a rich entrance into the eternal kingdom.

As we are contending for the faith,
enjoying the Blessed Trinity,
and taking the way of rapture
by giving heed to the prophetic word,
our trust is in our precious Lord
and God as the One who is able
to guard us from stumbling and
to set us before His glory
without blemish in exultation.

Living a Christian Life under the Government of God

Scripture Reading: 1 Pet. 1:17; 2:21-24; 4:17-19; 5:6

Day 1 I. **The Epistles of 1 and 2 Peter are on the universal government of God:**
   A. The subject of 1 Peter is the Christian life under the government of God, showing us the government of God especially in His dealings with His chosen people (1:2).
   B. The subject of 2 Peter is the divine provision and the divine government, showing us that as God is governing us, He supplies us with whatever we need (1:1-4; 3:13).
   C. God governs by judging; the judgment of God is for the carrying out of His government (1 Pet. 1:17; 4:17):
      1. Because 1 and 2 Peter are concerned with the government of God, in these Epistles the judgment of God and of the Lord is referred to repeatedly as one of the essential items (1 Pet. 2:23; 4:5-6, 17; 2 Pet. 2:3-4, 9; 3:7).
      2. Through various kinds of judgments, the Lord God will clear up the entire universe and purify it so that He may have a new heaven and a new earth for a new universe filled with His righteousness for His delight (v. 13).

Day 2 D. The judgment in 1 Peter 1:17, which is carried out by the Father, is not the future judgment but is the present, daily judgment of God's governmental dealings with His children:
      1. The Father has regenerated us to produce a holy family—a holy Father with holy children (vv. 3, 15, 17).
      2. As holy children, we should walk in a holy manner of life (vv. 15-16); otherwise, in His government God the Father will become

the Judge and will deal with our unholiness (4:15-17; Heb. 12:9-10).

E. The disciplinary judgment in the government of God begins from the house of God (1 Pet. 4:17): ＼

1. God judges everything that does not match His government; therefore, in this age we, the children of God, are under the daily judgment of God (1:17).

2. God uses fiery ordeals to deal with the believers in the judgment of His governmental administration, which begins from His own house (4:12, 17).

3. The purpose of this judgment is that we would live according to God in spirit (v. 6).

Day 3 II. **The preciousness of Peter's writings is that he combines the Christian life and God's government, revealing that the Christian life and the government of God go together as a pair (1 Pet. 1:17; 2:21, 24; 3:15; 4:17; 5:5-8):**

A. The Triune God has passed through a long process in Christ and has become the life-giving Spirit to indwell us; this is for our Christian life (John 1:14; 14:17; 1 Cor. 15:45b; 6:17).

B. At the same time, the Triune God is still the Creator of the universe and its Ruler (1 Pet. 4:19).

C. Although we have been born of God to have a spiritual life and to be a new creation, we are still in the old creation (John 1:12-13; 3:3, 5-6; 2 Cor. 5:17):

1. For this reason, we need God's governmental dealings (1 Pet. 1:17).

2. In order for the Christian life to grow, we need the discipline of God's government (2:2; 4:17; 2 Pet. 1:5-7).

Day 4 III. **When the Lord Jesus was on earth, He lived a human life that was absolutely under the government of God, and He committed** everything related to Him to God's government (John 6:38; 1 Pet. 2:21-23):

A. The Lord kept committing all His insults and injuries to Him who judges righteously in His government, the righteous God, to whom He submitted Himself; He put His trust in this righteous One, recognizing His government (v. 23).

B. When God counseled Christ as a man, Christ's inward parts were one with God and instructed Him through His contact with God (Psa. 16:7; Isa. 50:4).

IV. As believers in Christ and children of God, we should live a Christian life under the government of God (John 3:15; 1:12-13; 1 Pet. 4:13-19; 5:6-8):

A. The Epistles of Peter reveal the Christ who enables us to take God's governmental dealings administered through sufferings (1 Pet. 1:6-8; 2:3-4, 19, 21-25; 3:18, 22; 4:1, 15-16; 5:8-9).

B. We should pass the time of our sojourning in holy fear, that is, in a healthy, serious caution that leads us to be holy in all our manner of life (1:15, 17).

Day 5   C. We should be humbled under the mighty hand of God, which carries out the government of God (5:6):

1. In verse 6 the mighty hand of God refers to God's administrating hand seen especially in His judgment (1:17; 4:17).

2. To be humbled under God's mighty hand is to be made humble by God; however, we must cooperate with God's operation and be willing to be made humble, lowly, under His mighty hand (5:6).

Day 6   D. We should commit our souls to the faithful Creator (4:19):

1. God can preserve our soul, and His loving and faithful care accompanies His justice in His governmental administration.

    2. While God judges us in His government, He cares for us faithfully in His love; as we are suffering His disciplinary judgment, we should commit our souls to the faithful care of our Creator (Matt. 10:28; 11:28-29).

E. In the death of Christ we have died to sins so that in the resurrection of Christ we might live to righteousness under God's government (1 Pet. 2:24):

    1. God's government is established upon righteousness (Psa. 89:14a); as God's people living under His government, we must live a righteous life.

    2. The expression *live to righteousness* is related to the fulfilling of God's governmental requirements (1 Pet. 2:24):

        a. We were saved so that we might live rightly under the government of God, that is, in a way that matches the righteous requirements of His government.

        b. In Christ's death we have been separated from sins, and in His resurrection we have been enlivened so that in our Christian life we might live spontaneously to righteousness under the government of God (Rom. 6:8, 10-11, 18; Eph. 2:6; John 14:19; 2 Tim. 2:11).

Morning Nourishment

1 Pet. For it is time for the judgment to begin from the house
4:17 of God; and if first from us, what will be the end of
those who disobey the gospel of God?

In his two Epistles Peter is on the subject of God's universal government....Matthew is on the kingdom. Do not think that the
government and the kingdom are identical. No, the kingdom is
one thing and the government is another. A country or nation has
a government. The government, however, is not the nation; rather,
the government is the administrative center of the nation. For
example, the government in Washington, D.C., is the administrative center of the United States. Although Matthew presents the
kingdom, the government is not found in that book. The government of God is in the writings of Peter.

Mark presents service; Luke, salvation; and John, life. Thus, in
the four Gospels we have the kingdom, service, salvation, and life.
But we do not have the divine government. In his Epistles Peter
makes up this lack by showing us God's universal government.
(*Life-study of 1 Peter,* pp. 8-9)

Today's Reading

God's government covers the entire universe. We know this by
the fact that Peter speaks of the new heavens and new earth. This
indicates God's universal government. Eventually, in eternity
future, everything will be right and in good order, for righteousness will dwell in the new heavens and new earth. Today the
earth is filled with unrighteousness and disorder. Nevertheless,
God is still governing heaven and earth.

God governs by judging. This is the way God carries out His
government. As an elderly man who has some knowledge of
world history both by study and observation, I can testify that I
bow before God. He is the governing One, and He governs by judging. God has judged Hitler, Stalin, and other evildoers. On the one
hand, to some extent, God tolerated them in doing certain things
that served His purpose, such as Hitler's slaughtering of the Jews,
which caused the Jews to be one. Nevertheless, God judged them.

In 1 and 2 Peter we have a record of God's judgment. God judged the earth by means of the flood, the deluge. Later He judged Sodom and Gomorrah. The history of God's judgment also includes the judgment upon the children of Israel in the wilderness. During their years of wandering, the children of Israel experienced God's judgment again and again. With the exception of Joshua and Caleb, all those who came out of Egypt, including Moses, Aaron, and Miriam, died in the wilderness under God's judgment. Furthermore, the Bible says that thousands of the disobedient ones were strewn by God in the wilderness. That was God's judgment.

[Do] not think that God judges only evildoers such as Hitler and Stalin. God also judges His own people. According to 1 Peter 4:17, God's governing judgment begins from His own household.

What is the purpose of God's governing judgment? God judges in order to clear up His universe. The universe was created by God for a positive purpose, but Satan came in to defile it. Now God is cleansing the universe through judgment. He is doing a thorough work of cleaning the entire universe. Eventually, the universe will be new.

God will not live or dwell in a place that is unclean. Thus, God is cleansing, purifying, the universe. First He purifies us, His household....The reason we have difficulties is that God's judgment begins from His own household. You and I are under God's judgment.

The subject of 1 Peter, therefore, is the Christian life under the government of God. The subject of 2 Peter is a little different: it is the divine provision and the divine government. In his second Epistle Peter shows us that God is not only governing us, ruling us, but also providing us with whatever we need. God supplies us all things to live a holy life, a Christian life, under His government. (*Life-study of 1 Peter*, pp. 9-11)

Further Reading: Life-study of 1 Peter, msg. 1; *Life-study of 2 Peter,* msgs. 1, 9, 13; *A General Sketch of the New Testament in the Light of Christ and the Church, Part 3: Hebrews through Jude,* ch. 30

Enlightenment and inspiration: _____

_____

_____

_____

Morning Nourishment

1 Pet. But according to the Holy One who called you, you
1:15-17 yourselves also be holy in all *your* manner of life;
because it is written, "You shall be holy because I am
holy." And if you call *as* Father the One who without
respect of persons judges according to each one's
work, pass the time of your sojourning in fear.

First Peter 1:15 says, "But according to the Holy One who
called you, you yourselves also be holy in all your manner of
life."...In verse 16 Peter gives us the reason we need to be holy:
"Because it is written, You shall be holy because I am holy" [Lev.
11:44; 19:2; 20:7].

In 1 Peter 1:17 Peter continues, "And if you call upon as
Father the One who without respect of persons judges according
to each one's work, pass the time of your sojourning in fear." In
this verse Peter comes to the matter of God's government, the
particular point that he covers in his Epistles. The judgment of
God is for the carrying out of His government.

The Holy One who has called us as the Father has regenerated us to produce a holy family—a holy Father with holy
children. As holy children, we should walk in a holy manner of
life. Otherwise, the Father will become the Judge (4:17) to deal
with our unholiness. He begot us with life inwardly that we may
have His holy nature. He disciplines us with judgment outwardly that we may partake of His holiness (Heb. 12:9-10). His
judgment is according to our work, our conduct, without respect
of persons. Hence, we should pass the time of our sojourning in
fear. If we call upon Him as our Father, we should also fear Him
as our Judge and live a holy life in fear. (*Life-study of 1 Peter,*
pp. 91-92)

Today's Reading

In 1 Peter 1:17 Peter "is not speaking of the final judgment of
the soul. In that sense, the Father does not judge anyone, but He
has given all judgment to the Son (John 5:22). The thing spoken
of here is the daily judgment of God's government in this world,

exercised with regard to His children. Accordingly it says, 'the time of your sojourning' here" (Darby). This is God's judgment on His own household (1 Pet. 4:17).

Since these two Epistles are concerned with the government of God, the judgment of God and of the Lord is referred to repeatedly (2:23; 4:5-6, 17; 2 Pet. 2:3-4, 9; 3:7) as one of the essential items. It began from the angels (2 Pet. 2:3-4) and passed through the generations of man in the Old Testament (2 Pet. 2:5-9). Then in the New Testament age it begins from the house of God (1 Pet. 1:17; 2:23; 4:6, 17) and continues until the coming of the day of the Lord (2 Pet. 3:10), which will be a day of judgment on the Jews, the believers, and the Gentiles before the millennium. After the millennium, all the dead, including men and demons, will be judged and perish (1 Pet. 4:5; 2 Pet. 3:7), and the heavens and the earth will be burned up (2 Pet. 3:10b, 12). The results of the varied judgments are not the same. Some judgments result in a disciplinary dealing, some in a dispensational punishment, and some in eternal perdition. However, by all these judgments the Lord God will clear up the entire universe and purify it so that He may have a new heaven and a new earth for a new universe filled with His righteousness (2 Pet. 3:13) for His delight.

The daily judgment of God is not exercised upon fallen sinners; instead, it is exercised upon God's children....I am burdened that we all grasp the pure thought regarding [the truth of God's judgment] in the Bible. Today all of us are under God's judgment. God is not only gracing us, giving us grace. He is also judging us. This is the reason we have many sufferings. We have sufferings because God is judging us. On the one hand, God is gracing us to live a life that suits His righteousness under His government. On the other hand, He judges anything that does not match His government. Therefore, in this age we the believers are under the daily judgment of God. (*Life-study of 1 Peter,* pp. 92, 270)

Further Reading: Life-study of 1 Peter, msgs. 11, 30

Enlightenment and inspiration: _____

_____

_____

_____

Morning Nourishment

1 Pet. **Beloved, do not think that the fiery ordeal among**
4:12-13 **you, coming to you for a trial, is strange...but inas-**
much as you share in the sufferings of Christ,
rejoice, so that also at the revelation of His glory
you may rejoice exultingly.
2:21 **For to this you were called, because Christ also suf-**
fered on your behalf, leaving you a model so that
you may follow in His steps.

The Greek word for *fiery ordeal*...[in 1 Peter 4:12] means burning, signifying the burning of a smelting furnace for the purification of gold and silver (Prov. 27:21; Psa. 66:10), like the metaphor used in 1:7. Peter considered the persecution the believers suffered as such a burning furnace used by God to purify their life. This is God's way to deal with the believers in the judgment of His governmental administration, which begins from His own household (4:17-19)....Fiery persecution is common to the believers. They should not think it is strange or alien to them and be surprised and astonished by it. This persecution is a trial, a testing.

Peter's use of the metaphor of a burning furnace in verse 12 indicates that today the Lord is using persecutions and trials as a furnace to serve a positive purpose. The positive purpose served by persecution and trial is the purification of our life. We can be compared to gold and silver. However, we still have some amount of dross. Therefore, we need purification. As gold and silver are purified through burning, we also need to be purified in this way. In verse 12 Peter tells the believers not to regard the fiery ordeal as strange. As Christians, we should realize that fiery ordeals are common....It is our destiny to suffer in this age. Of course, this is not our eternal destiny. God has not destined us to suffer in eternity, but He surely has destined us to suffer in this age. (*Life-study of 1 Peter,* pp. 247-248)

Today's Reading

In 1 Peter 4:13 Peter...[indicates] that by experiencing such a fiery ordeal we share, participate in, the sufferings of Christ. Here

Peter is saying that it is possible for the sufferings a Christian undergoes to be the sufferings of Christ....If we were not Christians, we certainly would not suffer the kind of persecution described in verses 12 and 13. Such persecutions are due to the fact that we are Christians, men of Christ. Because we believe in Christ, love Christ, live Christ, bear testimony to Christ, witnessing of Him in this age, the world rises up against us. This age is under the hand of the evil one, and for this reason unbelieving ones persecute those who believe in Christ and witness of Him. In the sight of God this kind of suffering is regarded as the sufferings of Christ.

First Peter is a book on the Christian life under the government of God. It is easy for us to pay attention to the Christian life and to neglect God's government. Actually, the Christian life and the government of God go together. The Triune God has passed through a long process and has become the life-giving Spirit to indwell us. This is for our Christian life. At the same time, the Triune God is still the Creator of the universe and its ruler. On the one hand, we have been reborn to have a spiritual life, the divine life. On the other hand, we are still in the old creation. For this reason, we need God's governmental dealings. In order for the Christian life to grow, we need the discipline of God's government.

The preciousness of Peter's writings is that he combines the Christian life and God's government. Paul did the same thing, but he did not do it in such a clear way as Peter did. Peter's writings show us that the Christian life and the government of God go together as a pair. If we would carefully read the two Epistles of Peter, we would see that Peter is quite deep in the matter of life. The first chapter of 2 Peter, in particular, is rich, deep, and profound in the matter of life. But at the same time in his writings Peter gives a serious word regarding God's governmental dealings with His regenerated people. Therefore, in the Epistles of Peter we need to see the Christian life and God's government and also see how the two go together. (*Life-study of 1 Peter,* pp. 248-249, 280-281)

Further Reading: Life-study of 1 Peter, msgs. 27-28, 30-31

Enlightenment and inspiration: _____

_____

_____

_____

Morning Nourishment

1 Pet. ...Christ also suffered on your behalf...; who com-
2:21-24 mitted no sin, nor was guile found in His mouth;
who being reviled did not revile in return; suffer-
ing, He did not threaten but kept committing *all* to
Him who judges righteously; who Himself bore up
our sins in His body on the tree, in order that we,
having died to sins, might live to righteousness; by
whose bruise you were healed.

[In 1 Peter 2:23], according to the usage of the verb "kept committing" in Greek, "all" needs to be inserted here as its object. This word refers to all the sufferings of the Lord. He kept committing all the insults He suffered and all His injuries to Him who judges righteously in His government, to the righteous God, to whom He submitted Himself. This indicates that the Lord recognized God's government while He was living a human life on earth.

We are accustomed to saying that we commit things to the Lord who is faithful or merciful or kind. Have you ever said, "I commit everything to God who judges righteously"?...Our prayer, expression, and utterance are still too traditional. This keeps us from applying many of the thoughts and utterances in the pure Word. Therefore, in reading a verse such as 2:23, we may take it for granted and fail to get into the real meaning.

While the Lord Jesus was on earth suffering, He kept committing all to the One who judges righteously. This brief word indicates not only that the Lord lived a life that was a model for us, but also that He lived a life absolutely under God's government. He Himself was always under the government of God, and He committed everything related to Him to God's judgment. (*Life-study of 1 Peter*, pp. 185-186)

Today's Reading

In 1 Peter 1:17 Peter [says], "And if you call as Father the One who without respect of persons judges according to each one's work, pass the time of your sojourning in fear." In this verse Peter comes to the matter of God's government.... The judgment of God is for the carrying out of His government.

In verse 17 Peter urges us to pass the time of our sojourning in fear. This is a holy fear, as in Philippians 2:12. It refers to a healthy, serious caution for us to behave in a holy manner. Such fear is mentioned a number of times in this book because its teaching is concerning the government of God.

Verses 18 and 19 explain why we should pass the time of our sojourning in fear....Because we know that we have been redeemed by the precious blood of Christ...we now pass the time of our sojourning in fear. The point here is that the holy manner of life should issue out from the dear and precious redemption of Christ.

In order to pass the time of our sojourning in fear, we need a deep realization concerning the redemption of Christ. Today many Christians are living in a loose way because their understanding of Christ's redemption is shallow.

According to verse 18, the blood of Christ has redeemed us from our vain manner of life. This vain manner of life is in contrast to the holy manner of life in verse 15....Christ's redemption is for this—to separate us from our vain manner of life handed down from our fathers. Knowing that this was accomplished with the highest price, the precious blood of Christ, we pass the days of our sojourning in fear.

The blood of Christ, by which we are sprinkled and thus marked out from common people, is more precious than silver and gold. The highest price has been paid for our redemption, that we might be redeemed from the vain manner of life to the holy (vv. 18, 15). For this we should have a holy fear, a healthy, serious caution before God that, as God's elect, redeemed with such a high price, we would not miss the purpose of this most high redemption of Christ. (*Life-study of 1 Peter,* pp. 91-93, 97-99)

Further Reading: Life-study of 1 Peter, msgs. 21, 11-12

Enlightenment and inspiration: _____

_____

_____

_____

Morning Nourishment

1 Pet.   ...All of you gird yourselves with humility toward
5:5-6   one another, because God resists the proud but
        gives grace to the humble. Therefore be humbled
        under the mighty hand of God that He may exalt
        you in due time.

[According to 1 Peter 5:5] everyone in the church, including
the elders, should gird himself with humility....It is used here as a
figure of speech, signifying the putting on of humility as a virtue
in service. This figure comes evidently from Peter's impression of
how the Lord girded Himself with a towel when He humbled Himself to wash the disciples' feet, especially Peter's (John 13:4-7).

God resists the one who lifts himself above others and regards
himself as better than others. Instead of being proud and showing
ourselves above others, we should gird ourselves with the apron
of humility. Putting on such an apron will always bring us down
and cause us to be lowly.

The Greek word for "humble" in 5:5 also means lowly, as in
Matthew 11:29, where the Lord Jesus says, "I am meek and lowly
in heart." To be proud is to be high, but to be humble is to be low. If
we would humble ourselves in the church life, we need to become
lowly. Instead of uplifting ourselves, we should always keep ourselves low. Then we shall be in a position to receive the Triune
God as our life supply. We shall receive the grace God gives to
humble believers.

The words "be humbled" in 1 Peter 5:6 are in the passive voice,
indicating to be made humble by God, mainly through the sufferings in persecutions (v. 10). This, however, requires our cooperation with God's operation. We must be willing to be made humble,
lowly, under the mighty hand of God. Hence, *be humbled*. We may
say that "humbled" is passive, but "be" is active. While God is
acting to operate on us, we need to take the initiative to be operated on by Him. To take the initiative is active; to be operated on is
passive. This is our willingness to be under the hand of God,
which is mighty to do everything for us. (*Life-study of 1 Peter*,
pp. 297-299)

Today's Reading

Persecution may be used by God to humble us. Actually, any kind of suffering may be used by God for this purpose. When good things happen to us, we may become proud. But suffering or persecution may help us to be humble. For example, a brother may be humbled as a result of losing his job. A student may be humbled by receiving a lower grade than he expected.

We may also experience being humbled in our family life. If the children of a certain brother and sister are outstanding, the parents may become proud. But if the children cause them problems or difficulty, this will make the parents lowly.

In 1 Peter 5:6 Peter tells us to "be humbled." We cannot make ourselves humble. Rather, we need to be made humble by God. Nevertheless, God's humbling of us requires our cooperation with God's operation. This means that we must be willing to be made humble, lowly, under the mighty hand of God.

We may say that "be humbled" is active-passive: "be" is active, pointing to our initiative to be humbled, and "humbled" is passive, pointing to God's operation to humble us. Although God's hand is mighty to do whatever is necessary for us, His hand still needs our cooperation. God's operation needs our cooperation. Therefore, we need to be humbled.

The entire book of 1 Peter is on God's government, and that God's government is administrated through His judgment. God's judgment is carried out in the environment arranged according to His sovereignty. For example, in order to judge Noah's generation, God arranged a great catastrophe, the flood. Only God could have done such a thing. The flood that terminated the human race at the time of Noah was brought about by the mighty hand of God. In 5:6 the mighty hand of God refers to God's administrating hand seen especially in His judgment. (*Life-study of 1 Peter,* pp. 299-300, 307)

Further Reading: Life-study of 1 Peter, msgs. 33-34

Enlightenment and inspiration: _____

_____

_____

_____

Morning Nourishment

1 Pet. So then let those also who suffer according to the will
4:19 of God commit their souls in well-doing to a faithful
Creator.
2:24 Who Himself bore up our sins in His body on the tree,
in order that we, having died to sins, might live to
righteousness; by whose bruise you were healed.

The will of God in 1 Peter 4:19 is that He wants us to suffer for Christ's sake and has appointed us to this (3:17; 2:15; 1 Thes. 3:3). Literally, *commit* in 1 Peter 4:19 means to give in charge as a deposit....When the believers suffer persecution in their body, especially as in martyrdom, they should commit their souls as a deposit to God, the faithful Creator, as the Lord did with His spirit to the Father (Luke 23:46). The persecution could damage only the body of the suffering believers, not their souls (Matt. 10:28). Their souls are kept by the Lord as the faithful Creator. They should cooperate with the Lord by their faithful commitment....*Well-doing* indicates doing right, good, and noble deeds.

The Creator in verse 19 does not refer to the Creator of the new creation in the new birth, but to the Creator of the old creation. Persecution is a suffering in the old creation. God as our Creator can preserve our soul, which He created for us. He has even numbered our hairs (Matt. 10:30). He is loving and faithful. His loving and faithful care (1 Pet. 5:7) accompanies His justice in His governmental administration. While He is judging us, as His household, in His government, in His love He cares for us faithfully. In suffering His just disciplinary judgment in our body, we should commit our souls to His faithful care. (*Life-study of 1 Peter*, pp. 265-266)

Today's Reading

The phrase "having died to sins" [in 1 Peter 2:24] literally means being away from sins. When Christ carried up our sins onto the cross and died,...the death of Christ terminated us, and this termination can keep us away from sin. The best way for people to be kept from sins or from sin is for them to be put to death. No matter how many sins a person may commit, once he has died, death separates him from sins....Through Christ's death we can be kept away from sins so that we may live to righteousness. Apparently, being kept away from sin terminates us; actually, it enlivens us so that we may live to righteousness.

The life-giving Spirit is working within us continually to carry out the subjective aspect of Christ's cross in our being. Daily we are undergoing the inward working of the cross of Christ, and daily we are being made alive so that we may live to righteousness. Therefore, it is not difficult to overcome sins, because through Christ's death we are being kept away from sins....There is no need for us to strive or to try to energize ourselves. We simply live, and this living always has an inclination toward righteousness. This is the experience of our Savior saving us daily.

Peter uses the expression "live to righteousness."...Actually, God's government requires just one thing—righteousness. This is the reason 2 Peter 3:13 says, "But according to His promise we are expecting new heavens and a new earth, in which righteousness dwells." In 1 Peter 2:23 we see that the Lord Jesus continually committed all to the One who judges righteously. Then in verse 24 Peter indicates that we should live to righteousness. Peter's concept here is governmental; righteousness is a matter of God's government. We have been saved by our Savior to live a life that matches the righteous requirements of God's government.

God is righteous and His government is established upon righteousness. Psalm 89:14 says that righteousness is the foundation of God's throne....Because in ourselves we are not able to live this kind of life, the Savior saves us to live a life of righteousness, a life that fulfills the righteous requirements of God's government.... His death separates us from sins and enlivens us so that we may live to righteousness. Spontaneously, we are under God's government and have no problem with His government because we live to righteousness. (*Life-study of 1 Peter,* pp. 188-190)

Further Reading: Life-study of 1 Peter, msgs. 29, 21; *Life-study of 2 Corinthians,* msgs. 25, 27-29*

Enlightenment and inspiration: _____

_____

_____

Hymns, #21

1 We praise Thee for Thy righteousness;
   Thy justice, Father, we confess,
      And fully testify.
   Thou art the judge of all mankind,
   In Thee injustice none can find,
      Nor wrong to Thee apply.

2 O holy Father, righteous One,
   Thy righteousness upholds Thy throne,
      'Tis a foundation sure.
   'Tis through this righteousness of Thine
   That reigns in Christ the grace divine,
      And peace we thus secure.

3 Thy righteousness has caused Thy Son
   To die for us that we be won,
      Redemption thus was bought;
   Thy righteousness has justified
   When Christ's redemption was applied,
      Salvation thus was wrought.

4 That Thou might show Thy righteousness,
   With Thy forgiveness Thou didst bless
      Men in the ancient age;
   For Thee Thy righteousness to show,
   Remission Thou dost now bestow
      On sinners in this age.

5 All people Thou wilt judge one day,
   Thy righteousness to all display
      By Christ, Thy Son, our Lord;
   Yet fast we'll stand, for none can move,
   Thy righteousness we'll ever prove,
      With grace Thou wilt afford.

6 With justice is Thy kingdom filled,
   And peace upon it Thou dost build
      With all in harmony;
   In the new heaven and new earth
   Thy righteousness will be their worth,
      As promised, God, by Thee.

Composition for prophecy with main point and sub-points: _____

_____
_____
_____
_____
_____
_____
_____
_____
_____
_____
_____
_____
_____
_____
_____
_____
_____
_____
_____
_____
_____
_____
_____
_____
_____
_____
_____
_____
_____
_____
_____
_____
_____
_____
_____
_____
_____
_____

The Economy of God in 1 and 2 Peter

Scripture Reading: 1 Pet. 1:2-3, 5, 10-12, 20; 2:1-5, 9; 3:4; 4:14; 5:10; 2 Pet. 1:4; 3:13, 18

Day 1　I. In his two Epistles, comprising only eight chapters, Peter covered the entire economy of God, from eternity past before the foundation of the world (1 Pet. 1:2, 20) to the new heavens and the new earth in eternity future (2 Pet. 3:13); he unveiled the crucial things related to God's economy, concerning which things the prophets prophesied and the apostles preached (1 Pet. 1:10-12) from four sides:

A. From the side of the Triune God:

1. God the Father chose a people in eternity according to His foreknowledge (vv. 1-2; 2:9) and called them into His glory (5:10; 2 Pet. 1:3).

2. Christ, foreknown by God before the foundation of the world but manifested in the last times (1 Pet. 1:20), has redeemed and saved His chosen people (vv. 18-19, 2) by His vicarious death (2:24; 3:18) through His resurrection in life and ascension in power (1:3; 3:21-22).

3. The Spirit, sent from heaven, has sanctified and purified those whom Christ has redeemed (1:2, 12, 22; 4:14)—the angels long to look into these things (1:12).

Day 2　4. The Triune God's divine power has provided the redeemed ones with all things that relate to life and godliness (2 Pet. 1:3-4) to guard them unto full salvation (1 Pet. 1:5).

5. God also disciplines them (5:6) by some of His varied governmental judgments (1:17; 2:23; 4:5-6, 17; 2 Pet. 2:3-4, 9; 3:7), and He will perfect, establish, strengthen, and ground them by His all grace (1 Pet. 5:10).

6. The Lord is long-suffering toward them
   that they all may have opportunity to
   repent unto salvation (2 Pet. 3:9, 15).
7. Then, Christ will appear in glory with His
   full salvation for His lovers (1 Pet. 1:5, 7-9, 13;
   4:13; 5:4).

Day 3   B. From the side of the believers:
1. The believers, as God's possession, were
   chosen by God (1:2; 2:9), called by His glory
   and virtue (v. 9; 3:9; 2 Pet. 1:3, 10), redeemed
   by Christ (1 Pet. 1:18-19), regenerated by
   God through His living word (vv. 3, 23), and
   saved through the resurrection of Christ
   (3:21).
2. They now are being guarded by the power of
   God (1:5), are being purified to love one
   another (v. 22), are growing by feeding on
   the milk of the word (2:2), are developing in
   life the spiritual virtues (2 Pet. 1:5-8), and
   are being transformed and built up into a
   spiritual house, a holy priesthood to serve
   God (1 Pet. 2:4-5, 9).
3. They are God's chosen race, royal priesthood, holy nation, and peculiar people for
   His private possession to express His virtues (v. 9).
4. They are being disciplined by His governmental judgment (1:17; 2:19-21; 3:9, 14, 17;
   4:6, 12-19; 5:6, 9), are living a holy life in
   an excellent manner and in godliness to
   glorify Him (1:15; 2:12; 3:1-2), are ministering as good stewards of His varied
   grace for His glorification through Christ
   (4:10-11)—under the elders' exemplary
   shepherding (5:1-4)—and are expecting
   and hastening the coming of the Lord (1:13;
   2 Pet. 3:12) in order to be richly supplied
   with an entrance into the eternal kingdom
   of the Lord (1:11).

Day 4

Day 5 & Day 6

5. Further, they are expecting the new heavens and new earth, in which righteousness dwells, in eternity (3:13), and they are growing continually in the grace and knowledge of our Lord and Savior Jesus Christ (v. 18).

C. From the side of Satan—Satan is the believers' adversary, the devil, who as a roaring lion is walking about, seeking someone to devour (1 Pet. 5:8).

D. From the side of the universe:
   1. The fallen angels were condemned and are awaiting eternal judgment (2 Pet. 2:4); the ancient ungodly world was destroyed by a flood (v. 5; 3:6); the ungodly cities were reduced to ashes (2:6); the false teachers and heretical mockers in the apostasy and mankind in his evil living will all be judged unto destruction (vv. 1, 3, 9-10, 12; 3:3-4, 7; 1 Pet. 4:5); the heavens and the earth will be burned up (2 Pet. 3:7, 10-11); and all the dead men and the demons will be judged (1 Pet. 4:5).
   2. Then the new heavens and new earth will come as a new universe, in which God's righteousness will dwell for eternity (2 Pet. 3:13).

II. **The central focus and basic structure of 1 and 2 Peter are the energizing Triune God operating in His economy to bring His chosen ones into the full enjoyment of the Triune God; our human spirit, as the hidden man of the heart, and God's Spirit, as the Spirit of glory and as the Spirit of Christ, are the means for us to partake of God, in His divine nature, as our portion (1 Pet. 1:2-3, 5, 11; 2:1-3, 5, 9; 3:4; 4:14; 5:10; 2 Pet. 1:4):**

A. Although the subject of 1 and 2 Peter is God's government, this is not the central focus and

basic structure of these Epistles; everything
concerning God's government should bring us
back to the central focus and basic structure of
these Epistles—the Triune God as our full
enjoyment.

B. The central focus and basic structure of 1 and
2 Peter are the Triune God operating to accomplish His complete salvation so that we may be
regenerated, so that we may feed on His word,
and so that we may grow, be transformed, and be
built up in order that He may have a dwelling
place and in order that we may be glorified to
express Him (1 Pet. 1:23; 2:1-5, 9).

C. Peter was bold in admitting that the early apostles, such as John, Paul, and himself (although
their style, terminology, utterance, certain
aspects of their views, and the way they presented their teachings differed), participated in
the same, unique ministry, the ministry of the
New Testament (2 Pet. 1:12-21; 3:2, 15-16; 2 Cor.
3:6, 8-9; 4:1).

D. Such a ministry ministers to people, as its focus,
the all-inclusive Christ as the embodiment of
the Triune God, who, after passing through the
processes of incarnation, human living, crucifixion, resurrection, and ascension, dispenses
Himself through the redemption of Christ and
by the operation of the Holy Spirit into His
redeemed people as their unique portion of life
and as their life supply and everything, for the
building up of the church as the Body of Christ,
which will consummate in the full expression,
the fullness, of the Triune God, according to the
eternal purpose of the Father (Acts 2:36;
3:13, 15; 10:36; 1 Pet. 1:2-3, 18-19, 23; 2:2-5, 7,
9, 25; 3:7; 4:10, 17; 5:2, 4, 10; 2 Pet. 1:2-4; 3:18).

Morning Nourishment

1 Pet. Chosen according to the foreknowledge of God the
1:2 Father in the sanctification of the Spirit unto the obedience and sprinkling of the blood of Jesus Christ...

2:24 Who Himself bore up our sins in His body on the tree,
in order that we, having died to sins, might live to
righteousness; by whose bruise you were healed.

3:18 For Christ also has suffered once for sins, the Righteous on behalf of the unrighteous, that He might
bring you to God, on the one hand being put to death
in the flesh, but on the other, made alive in the Spirit.

In his two Epistles of only eight chapters Peter has covered the
entire economy of God, from eternity past before the foundation of
the world (1 Pet. 1:2, 20) to the new heavens and new earth in
eternity future (2 Pet. 3:13). He unveils the crucial things related
to God's economy, which the prophets prophesied and the apostles
preached (1 Pet. 1:10-12), from four sides: [from the side of the
Triune God, of the believers, of Satan, and of the universe].

From the side of the Triune God, God the Father has chosen a
people in eternity according to His foreknowledge (1 Pet. 1:1-2; 2:9)
and has called them to His glory (1 Pet. 5:10; 2 Pet. 1:3). Christ, foreknown by God before the foundation of the world, but manifested in
the last times, has redeemed God's chosen people (1 Pet. 1:18-19, 2)
by His vicarious death (1 Pet. 2:24; 3:18) through His resurrection
in life and ascension in power (1 Pet. 1:3; 3:21-22). The Spirit, sent
from heaven, has sanctified and purified those whom Christ has
redeemed (1 Pet. 1:2, 12, 22; 4:14). (Life-study of 2 Peter, pp. 116-117)

Today's Reading

First Peter 1:2 shows us the working of the Divine Trinity:...
the foreknowledge of God the Father, the sanctification of the
Spirit, and the sprinkling of the blood of Jesus Christ [the Son].
The Father as the source foreknew us.... [Then] the Spirit came to
sanctify us...to separate us and bring us back to God. This is the
aspect of the Holy Spirit's sanctification before Christ's redemption. Then there is the sprinkling of the blood of Jesus Christ, the

Son, indicating Christ's redemption. The sanctification of the Spirit is divided into three stages. The first is for our repentance, the second is for our justification, and the third is for our transformation. In the book of Romans, Christ's redemption is revealed first and then the Holy Spirit's sanctification. But in 1 Peter 1:2 the sanctification of the Spirit is first, and then the sprinkling of the blood of Jesus Christ follows this sanctification. This is why we need to see the different aspects and stages of the sanctification of the Spirit.

In Luke 15 the Lord Jesus told three parables....These three parables reveal the Divine Trinity. The Son is the good shepherd, the Holy Spirit is the seeking woman, and God the Father is the loving and receiving father....The seeking woman lights a lamp, sweeps the house, and seeks carefully until she finds her lost coin (vv. 8, 10, 17). This typifies the sanctifying work of the Holy Spirit. He enlightens us from within and searches out our sins one by one that we may know our sins and repent.

Before we received the Lord, we were living in the world with the worldly people. But one day the Spirit came to find us....He sanctified us, separated us unto God, before we were forgiven of our sins and justified by God the Father. His sanctifying work separated us unto God so that we would come to ourselves (Luke 15:17), repent, and turn to God (Acts 26:20).

The seeking of the woman in Luke 15 typifies the initial sanctification of the Spirit which is the sanctification of the Spirit revealed in 1 Peter 1:2. Thus, we can see that 1 Peter 1:2 unveils the divine economy through the operation of the Trinity of the Godhead for the believers' participation in the Triune God. God the Father's selection is the initiation; God the Spirit's sanctification carries out the selection of God the Father; and God the Son's redemption, signified by the sprinkling of His blood, is the completion. (*Living in and with the Divine Trinity*, pp. 37-38)

Further Reading: Living in and with the Divine Trinity, ch. 4; *The Spirit with Our Spirit*, ch. 9; *God's New Testament Economy*, ch. 18

Enlightenment and inspiration: _____

_____
_____
_____

Morning Nourishment

2 Pet. Seeing that His divine power has granted to us all
1:3-4 things which relate to life and godliness, through the
full knowledge of Him who has called us by His own
glory and virtue, through which He has granted to us
precious and exceedingly great promises that
through these you might become partakers of the
divine nature, having escaped the corruption which
is in the world by lust.

1 Pet. But the God of all grace, He who has called you into
5:10 His eternal glory in Christ Jesus, after you have suffered a little while, will Himself perfect, establish,
strengthen, *and* ground *you.*

At the beginning of his second Epistle Peter speaks concerning
the divine provision. He tells us that the divine power has granted
us and even imparted to us all things related to life and godliness
in order that we may partake of the divine nature. Furthermore,
according to chapter one of 2 Peter, the divine provision gives us
not only the divine life but also the divine light (v. 19).

At the end of his first Epistle Peter says, "But the God of all
grace, He who has called you into His eternal glory in Christ Jesus,
after you have suffered a little while, will Himself perfect, establish, strengthen, and ground you" (5:10). Here Peter indicates that
we shall be grounded in God Himself. Then at the end of his
second Epistle Peter says, "But grow in the grace and knowledge
of our Lord and Savior Jesus Christ" (3:18). Here the knowledge of
our Lord is equal to the truth, the reality of all that He is. Therefore, in this verse Peter charges us to grow in grace and in truth,
reality. Although Peter covers many matters in his Epistles, the
basic structure of his writings is the Triune God becoming our
grace that we may enjoy Him, grow in life, and through the
growth in life be perfected, established, strengthened, and
grounded in the Triune God. (*Life-study of Jude,* pp. 27-28)

Today's Reading

Second Peter 1:1 speaks of the equally precious faith allotted to us, which is the same faith that Peter had. Then verse 3 speaks of the divine power within us, which has granted to us all things which relate to life within and godliness without, and verse 4 speaks of precious and exceedingly great promises. Finally, verse 4 says that we are partakers of the divine nature. If we have these six items—precious faith, divine power, life, godliness, precious promises, and the divine nature—what else could we desire?

We can never be rid of this precious faith within us. When we are under trials and temptations, we may say that it is no good to try to be a Christian. We simply cannot make it, so we try to drop being a Christian. However, we cannot drop it. We may try to drop the Lord, but He will not drop us; the precious faith grabs hold of us. Because there is something living within us, which is precious faith, the more we try to drop the Lord, the more He lays hold of us. This is truly mysterious. This precious faith within us is the strongest confirmation that we have been chosen by God.

It is from this living faith within us that we have the divine power. Today many people are seeking the outward power of the baptism in the Holy Spirit. However, real power is not outward but inward. We may illustrate this with atomic power. Atomic power is not merely outward; it is contained within even the poorest natural materials. Within us there is a divine "atomic" power. This divine power has granted to us all things which relate to life and godliness. Life is the content within, and godliness is our living without.

We have everything we need. God takes care of us in such a full and complete way. He knows our true condition, so He gives us many precious promises that through them we might become partakers of His divine nature to be the same as He is in nature. How wonderful this is! (*A General Sketch of the New Testament in the Light of Christ and the Church, Part 3: Hebrews through Jude*, p. 333)

Further Reading: Life-study of 2 Peter, msg. 13; *Life-study of Jude,* msg. 4

Enlightenment and inspiration: _____

_____

_____

_____

Morning Nourishment

1 Pet. **Blessed be the God and Father of our Lord Jesus**
1:3-5 **Christ, who according to His great mercy has regen-**
erated us unto a living hope through the resurrec-
tion of Jesus Christ from the dead, unto an inheri-
tance, incorruptible and undefiled and unfading,
kept in the heavens for you, who are being guarded
by the power of God through faith unto a salvation
ready to be revealed at the last time.
2 Pet. **For in this way the entrance into the eternal king-**
1:11 **dom of our Lord and Savior Jesus Christ will be**
richly *and* bountifully supplied to you.

[Of the four crucial things related to God's economy, the second is from the side of the believers.] The believers, as God's possession, were chosen by God (1 Pet. 1:1-2; 2:9), called by His glory and virtue (1 Pet. 2:9; 3:9; 2 Pet. 1:3, 10), redeemed by Christ (1 Pet. 1:18-19), regenerated by God through His living word (vv. 3, 23), and saved through the resurrection of Christ (3:21). They now are being guarded by the power of God (1:5), are being purified to love one another (v. 22), are growing by feeding on the milk of the word (2:2), are developing in life the spiritual virtues (2 Pet. 1:5-8), and are being transformed and built up into a spiritual house, a holy priest-hood to serve God (1 Pet. 2:4-5, 9). They are God's chosen race, royal priesthood, holy nation, and peculiar people for His private posses-sion to express His virtues (v. 9). They are being disciplined by His governmental judgment (1:17; 2:19-21; 3:9, 14, 17; 4:6, 12-19; 5:6, 9), are living a holy life in an excellent manner and in godliness to glorify Him (1:15; 2:12; 3:1-2), are ministering as good stewards of His varied grace for His glorification through Christ (4:10-11) (under the elders' exemplary shepherding—5:1-4), and are expect-ing and hastening the coming of the Lord (1:13; 2 Pet. 3:12) in order to be richly supplied with an entrance into the eternal kingdom of the Lord (1:11). Further, they are expecting the new heavens and new earth, in which righteousness dwells, in eternity (3:13), and they are growing continually in the grace and knowledge of our Lord and Savior Jesus Christ (v. 18). (2 Pet. 3:16, footnote 2)

Today's Reading

[First Peter 1:1—2:11 reveals that] God in eternity past selected us according to His foreknowledge to be His chosen people....God selected us for a purpose,...that God would put Himself into us as our life so that we may grow with Him into a building, His dwelling place....Furthermore, this building becomes God's expression to "tell out the virtues of Him" as the One who has called us out of darkness into His marvelous light (2:9). To tell out God's virtues is to express what He is. This is God's purpose. This is also God's goal.

If God would fulfill His purpose and reach His goal, He needs to apply to us what He decided in eternity past. In order to do this, it is necessary for God to be the Spirit. It is the Spirit who applies to us what God has decided. Moreover, because His chosen people had become fallen, it became necessary for God to accomplish redemption....In 1 Peter we see that the Spirit applies God's decision to us, the Son redeems us, and the Father regenerates us (1:3)....God entered into us as the divine life containing the divine "genes" to regenerate us. Now that we have been regenerated, we may taste that the Lord is good (2:3). (*Life-study of Jude,* p. 30)

Faith [2 Peter 1:1] may be compared to a root and the divine power [v. 3], to a sprout. Then out of this comes a tree with fruit, which are the virtues which grow out of faith. Verse 5 speaks of adding, bringing in beside. This means that beside the six items in verses 1 to 4—precious faith, divine power, life, godliness, precious promises, and the divine nature—we must add all the virtues in verses 5 to 7. By the divine power and divine nature, virtue grows out as the issue of faith....This growth begins from faith and issues in love, like the growth of the tree of life. (*A General Sketch of the New Testament in the Light of Christ and the Church, Part 3: Hebrews through Jude,* p. 334)

Further Reading: Life-study of Jude, msg. 4; *A General Sketch of the New Testament in the Light of Christ and the Church, Part 3: Hebrews through Jude,* ch. 30

Enlightenment and inspiration: _____

_____

_____

_____

Morning Nourishment

1 Pet. Be sober; watch. Your adversary, the devil, as a roar-
5:8-9 ing lion, walks about, seeking someone to devour.
Him withstand, being firm in your faith, knowing
that the same sufferings are being accomplished
among your brotherhood in the world.

2 Pet. Expecting and hastening the coming of the day of
3:12-13 God, on account of which the heavens, being on fire,
will be dissolved, and the elements, burning with
intense heat, are to be melted away. But according to
His promise we are expecting new heavens and a
new earth, in which righteousness dwells.

[Of the four crucial things related to God's economy, the third is
from the side of Satan.] Satan is the believers' adversary, the devil, as
a roaring lion walking about, seeking someone to devour (1 Pet. 5:8).

[The fourth is from the side of the universe.] The fallen angels
were condemned for eternal judgment (2 Pet. 2:4); the ancient
ungodly world was destroyed by a flood (v. 5; 3:6); the ungodly
cities were reduced to ashes (2:6); the false teachers and heretical
mockers in the apostasy and the living mankind will all be judged
unto destruction (v. 1, 3, 9-10, 12; 3:3-4, 7; 1 Pet. 4:5); the heavens
and the earth will be burned up (2 Pet. 3:7,10, 11); and all the dead
men and the demons will be judged (1 Pet. 4:5). Then the new
heavens and the new earth will come as a new universe, in which
God's righteousness will dwell for eternity (2 Pet. 3:13). (*Life-
study of 2 Peter*, p. 118)

Today's Reading

We need to see the central focus of [1 and 2 Peter and Jude]....
In 1 Peter actually only one and a half chapters are crucial in relation to life....[This includes] all of chapter one and the first eleven
verses of chapter two. In addition, we need to regard Peter's word
in 5:10 as crucial....We have a similar situation in...2 Peter. In
this book the first half of the first chapter and the last verse of the
last chapter are crucial in relation to life. In these vital portions of
1 and 2 Peter we have the central focus of these Epistles.

In 1 Peter 1:2 we see the foreknowledge of God the Father, the sanctification of the Spirit, and the sprinkling of the blood of Jesus Christ. This verse reveals the Father's foreknowledge, the Son's redemption, and the Spirit's application. This is the operation of the Triune God to carry out God's full salvation. In verse 3 Peter says that the Father has regenerated us unto a living hope. The full salvation of God is composed of three elements: the Father's regeneration, the Son's redemption, and the Spirit's application. When we experience this salvation, we have a life that is characterized by holiness and love. We are holy in our manner of life, and we love the brothers. Therefore, holiness and love are the issue of God's full salvation. Furthermore, in this salvation there is a seed, the incorruptible seed, which is the living and abiding word of God. This is a simple sketch of chapter one of 1 Peter.

Let us now go on to consider 1 Peter 2:1-11. Having been regenerated, we are now newborn babes longing for the guileless milk of the word so that by it we may grow unto salvation (v. 2). In chapter one we see that we have been regenerated and that the full salvation of God is our portion. Now we need to partake of and enjoy this salvation. For this, we need to feed on the milk of the word.

By feeding on the guileless milk of the word and by growing unto salvation, we shall be transformed into precious stones. Therefore, Peter refers to the believers as living stones (v. 5). These stones are for the building up of a spiritual house, and this house is a holy priesthood: "You yourselves also, as living stones, are being built up as a spiritual house into a holy priesthood to offer up spiritual sacrifices acceptable to God through Jesus Christ" (v. 5). On the one hand, this spiritual house is God's dwelling place; on the other hand, it is something that tells out the virtues of God, that expresses what God is [v. 9]. This spiritual house, of course, is a corporate matter. We are being built up together in a corporate way to afford God a dwelling place and to tell out God's virtues, that is, to express Him. (*Life-study of Jude*, pp. 38-40)

Further Reading: Life-study of Jude, msg. 5

Enlightenment and inspiration: _____

_____

_____

_____

Morning Nourishment

1 Pet. Let your adorning not be the outward,...but the
3:3-4 hidden man of the heart in the incorruptible *adorn-ment* of a meek and quiet spirit, which is very costly in the sight of God.

4:14 If you are reproached in the name of Christ, you are blessed, because the Spirit of glory and of God rests upon you.

1:11 Searching into what *time* or what manner of time the Spirit of Christ in them was making clear, testifying beforehand of the sufferings of Christ and the glories after these.

[Peter unveils that the] Triune God is our portion. This fact is indicated by the word "partakers" in 2 Peter 1:4. According to this verse, we have become partakers of the divine nature. This indicates that the Triune God is now our portion. If God were not our portion, we could not partake of His nature.

In his writings Peter also reveals the way for us to partake of the Triune God as our portion. The way involves the hidden man of the heart, and this hidden man is our spirit (1 Pet. 3:4). In his Epistles Paul has much to say concerning our spirit, but he does not use the expression "the hidden man of the heart." This hidden man, our human spirit, is the means by which we enjoy the Triune God as our portion.

Although Peter speaks of God's Spirit only a few times, his terminology is marvelous. In 1 Peter 4:14 he says, "If you are reproached in the name of Christ, you are blessed, because the Spirit of glory and of God rests upon you."...The Spirit of glory is the Spirit of God. Peter also speaks concerning the Spirit of Christ (1 Pet. 1:11). Our human spirit as the hidden man of the heart and God's Spirit as the Spirit of glory and as the Spirit of Christ are the means for us to partake of God as our portion. (*Life-study of Jude*, p. 26)

Today's Reading

We have pointed out that the Epistles of Peter are on the subject of God's government, in particular on God's governmental dealings through judgment. This is the central subject of these two books. Nevertheless, the structure of 1 and 2 Peter is the Triune God, who has been processed to become our portion so that we may participate in Him, partake of Him, and enjoy Him through His Spirit, who is the Spirit of Christ and the Spirit of glory, and by the exercise of our spirit.

I encourage you to study all the details in the Epistles of Peter. However, as you study these details, do not be distracted from the central thought and the basic structure of God's holy writings in general and the Epistles of Peter in particular. The basic structure is the Triune God who has been processed to become our all-inclusive portion. We enjoy Him by exercising our spirit to cooperate with and respond to the divine Spirit. We should never forget this basic structure or be distracted from it. If we hold firmly to the basic thought and the basic structure as we study all the other points in the writings of Peter, we shall be enriched and we shall experience the Triune God in a very rich, absolute, and detailed way.

The three Epistles of 1 and 2 Peter and Jude cover many points. But the basic structure of these Epistles is the Triune God operating on His elect that they may be brought into the full enjoyment of the Triune God. Both Peter and Jude indicate strongly that the Triune God has passed through a process in order to do many things for us and to become everything to us that we may partake of Him for our enjoyment.

As we study the details of the Epistles of Peter and Jude, we need to remember that all the detailed points help us to solve our problems so that we may be brought back to the enjoyment of the Triune God. Therefore, we should not consider the details in a detached way. Every point is a help in solving our problems so that we would not be distracted further from the enjoyment of the Triune God, but instead be brought back to this enjoyment. (*Life-study of Jude*, pp. 27-28)

Further Reading: Life-study of Jude, msg. 4; *The Divine Dispensing of the Divine Trinity*, ch. 9

Enlightenment and inspiration: _____

_____

_____

_____

Morning Nourishment

2 Pet. And count the long-suffering of our Lord *to be* salva-
3:15-16 tion, even as also our beloved brother Paul, according
to the wisdom given to him, wrote to you, as also in all
his letters, speaking in them concerning these things,
in which some things are hard to understand, which
the unlearned and unstable twist, as also the rest of
the Scriptures, to their own destruction.

Paul in his writings also spoke concerning "these things" [2 Pet.
3:16].... Hence, Peter referred to Paul's writings to strengthen his
own writings, especially concerning God's governmental and disciplinary judgment upon the believers. Paul strongly and repeatedly emphasized this matter in his writings (1 Cor. 11:30-32; Heb.
12:5-11; 2:3; 4:1; 6:8; 10:27-31, 39; 12:29; 1 Cor. 3:13-15; 4:4-5;
2 Cor. 5:10; Rom. 14:10).

What beauty and excellency are in this commendation!
Although the Corinthians attempted to divide Peter and Paul
according to their divisive preferences (1 Cor. 1:11-12), Peter com-
mended Paul, saying that Paul, like him, taught "these things"
and that Paul's writings should not be twisted but should be
regarded like "the rest of the Scriptures" and should receive the
same respect as the Old Testament....Peter was bold in admitting
that the early apostles, such as John, Paul, and himself, although
their style, terminology, utterance, certain aspects of their views,
and the way they presented their teachings differed, participated
in the same, unique ministry, the ministry of the New Testament
(2 Cor. 3:8-9; 4:1). Such a ministry ministers to people, as its focus,
the all-inclusive Christ as the embodiment of the Triune God,
who, after passing through the process of incarnation, human
living, crucifixion, resurrection, and ascension, dispenses Himself
through the redemption of Christ and by the operation of the
Holy Spirit into His redeemed people as their unique portion of
life and as their life supply and everything, for the building up of
the church as the Body of Christ, which will consummate in the
full expression, the fullness, of the Triune God, according to the
eternal purpose of the Father. (2 Pet. 3:16, footnote 2)

Today's Reading

In 2 Peter 3:16 Peter says that the unlearned and unstable twist Paul's writings and also the rest of the Scriptures, to their own destruction. This indicates that the mockers (2 Pet. 3:3) and their followers must have twisted the Scriptures and the apostles' teachings.

According to the context, "destruction" in verse 16 refers not to eternal perdition, but to the punishment of the divine governmental discipline. (*Life-study of 2 Peter,* p. 119)

The heart of 1 Peter is the operation of the Triune God to carry out His threefold salvation, which includes regeneration, redemption, and application. We have become God's children through regeneration, and now we need to feed on His word in order to grow unto full salvation. Then we shall be transformed in order to be built together to provide God a dwelling place and to be His expression. For this purpose, the God of all grace will perfect, establish, strengthen, and ground us. Furthermore, according to 2 Peter 3:18, we need to grow in God's grace and in the knowledge of Him. This is the focus of 1 and 2 Peter and...Jude.

[The] basic structure [of these books] is the Triune God operating to accomplish a threefold salvation so that we may be regenerated, that we may feed on His word, and that we may grow, be transformed, and be built up in order that He may have a dwelling place and that we may express Him.

This basic thought can also be seen in the Epistles of Paul... (2 Pet. 3:15-16). Paul also reveals that we may feed on the Lord and grow in order to be built up into a spiritual house so that God may have a corporate expression. Therefore, these two apostles ministered the same thing, but with somewhat different terminology. Both Peter and Paul had the same focus. I hope that none of us in the Lord's recovery will be distracted from the central focus and the basic structure of the apostles' ministry revealed in the New Testament. (*Life-study of Jude,* pp. 40-41)

Further Reading: Life-study of Jude, msg. 5

Enlightenment and inspiration: _____

_____

_____

Hymns, #1211

1   Given us, given us, God has given us
    Precious faith, power divine, greatest promises.
    We believed, we received, now we have all three;
    By these we may grow unto maturity.

2   Precious faith in each saint, precious equally,
    Precious faith holding us, holding ceaselessly.
    Disagree or agree, still it holds us fast,
    Day by day, eternally this faith shall last.

3   Power divine wrought in us is the source so great;
    Power divine is in us now to operate.
    Hence will spring everything for our life within
    And for godliness without, expressing Him.

4   Promises, promises, all God's called ones share;
    Promises, given us, great and precious are.
    These we take to partake of God's nature true,
    Having thus escaped the world's corruption too.

5   Christ within, as the pow'r, in our spirit lives;
    Christ without is the Word—all God's promises.
    Now the key is that we daily contact both,
    Calling, praying, reading to produce the growth.

6   Faith and pow'r, promises—these our full supply.
    Diligence, diligence, let us now apply;
    For if we, to these three, full attention show
    From the seed of faith the fruit of love will grow.

7   In the growth from the seed many items come;
    By this growth in the Lord fruitful we become.
    For this we need to see what the Lord's begun,
    Ne'er forgetful be nor blind to what He's done.

8   Diligence day by day will this growth insure;
    Diligence thus will make our election sure.
    When indeed with this seed we cooperate,
    We're supplied the kingdom's entrance, rich and great.

9   For this growth, for this growth, Lord, ourselves we give,
    By the faith, promises, and the pow'r to live.
    Nothing more, nothing less, will our basis be
    By Thy grace we will cooperate with Thee.

Composition for prophecy with main point and sub-points: _____

_____

_____

_____

_____

_____

_____

_____

_____

_____

_____

_____

_____

_____

_____

_____

_____

_____

_____

_____

_____

_____

_____

_____

_____

_____

_____

_____

_____

_____

_____

_____

_____

_____

_____

_____

_____

The Operation of the Triune God

Scripture Reading: 1 Pet. 1:2-4, 15, 23; 2:19; 4:6; 2 Pet. 1:2, 8; 3:18

Day 1   I. **Chapter 1 of 1 Peter, especially verses 2 and 3, reveals the energetic operation of the Triune God to bring God's chosen ones into the participation in the Triune God and into the full enjoyment of Himself:**

A. The Triune God passed through a process to do many things for us and become everything to us so that we may partake of Him for our enjoyment (vv. 18-20, 3).

B. The believers were chosen by God the Father before the foundation of the world, in eternity past; this was done according to the Father's foreknowledge and is carried out in time in the sanctification of the Spirit unto the obedience and sprinkling of the blood of Jesus Christ (v. 2; Eph. 1:4):

1. To foreknow is to foreordain, to ordain beforehand (Rom. 8:29).

2. First Peter 1:20 says that Christ was foreknown, foreordained, and verse 2 says that the believers were chosen according to the foreknowledge, the foreordination, of God; thus, verse 20 matches verse 2:

a. For Christ to be foreknown before the foundation of the world means that He was foreordained by God (v. 20).

b. The foreknowledge of God in verse 2 implies that in eternity past God approved us, appreciated us, and possessed us.

c. At the same time that God foreknew and foreordained Christ, He also foreknew and foreordained all the believers (vv. 20, 2).

Day 2   C. God the Spirit's sanctification carries out God the Father's selection (v. 2):

1. In eternity God chose us, making a decision to

gain us; in time the Spirit comes to sanctify us,
to set us apart, from the world so that we
would obey Christ's redemption (Eph. 1:4-5).

2. The sanctification of God the Spirit separates
us from the world and causes us to come to
ourselves, repent, and turn to God so that we
may belong to Him and enjoy His full salvation (Luke 15:17; John 16:8-11; Acts 20:21;
26:18, 20; Rom. 5:10).

3. In 1 Peter 1:2 the sanctification of the Spirit
comes before obedience to Christ and faith in
His redemption, indicating that the believers'
obedience unto faith in Christ results from the
Spirit's sanctifying work (Rom. 1:5).

Day 3   D. The issue of the Spirit's sanctification is our participation in the sprinkling of the blood of Jesus
Christ, which is the application of redemption
(1 Pet. 1:2):

1. The sanctification of the Spirit brought us to the
blood shed by the Savior on the cross and separated us unto this divine provision (vv. 18-19).

2. The sprinkling of Christ's redeeming blood
brings the sprinkled believers into the blessing of the new covenant, that is, into the full
enjoyment of the Triune God (Heb. 9:13-14).

3. The first thing in God's salvation is to sprinkle
us with the blood of the second of the Trinity;
thus, we are washed, forgiven, justified, and
reconciled to God (1 Cor. 6:11; Rom. 5:10).

4. In 1 Peter 1:2 obedience implies repentance
and faith; the sanctification of the Spirit is
unto the obedience of repentance and believing; thus, our repentance and believing into
Christ result from the Spirit's sanctifying
work (Acts 11:18; John 3:15; 1 Pet. 1:8).

E. Because of God's choosing, the Spirit's sanctifying,
and Christ's redeeming, God the Father has regenerated us through the resurrection of Jesus Christ
from the dead (v. 3):

  1. When God regenerated us, He put Christ into us as our life so that we may have the divine life in addition to our human life and have a relationship of life with God (John 1:12-13; 3:3, 6, 15; 11:25; Rom. 8:16).

  2. We were regenerated through the living and abiding word of God as the incorruptible seed containing God's life (1 Pet. 1:23).

Day 4 F. The threefold description of our inheritance points to the Trinity (v. 4):

  1. *Incorruptible* refers to the nature of the inheritance; this is God's nature, signified by gold (v. 7).

  2. *Undefiled* describes the condition of the inheritance; this condition is related to the sanctifying Spirit.

  3. *Unfading* refers to the expression of the inheritance; this everlasting expression is related to the Son as the expression of the Father's glory.

  G. The Spirit of Christ is the Spirit of God constituted through and with the death and resurrection of Christ for the application and impartation of Christ's death and resurrection to the believers (v. 11; John 7:39; Phil. 1:19):

  1. Although the constituting of the Spirit of Christ is dispensational, constituted dispensationally through and with Christ's death and resurrection in the New Testament time, His function is eternal, because He is the eternal Spirit (Heb. 9:14).

  2. According to function, there is no difference between the Spirit's work in the prophets and His work in the apostles (1 Pet. 1:10, 12).

Day 5 H. The Holy One who called us is the Triune God—the choosing Father, the redeeming Son, and the sanctifying Spirit; the Father regenerated us, the Son redeemed us, and the Spirit sanctifies us so that we may be holy in all our manner of life (vv. 2-3, 15-16, 18-19).

II. **To bless God is to speak well concerning the Triune God and all that He is to us, has done for us, and will do for us (v. 3):**
   A. To bless God is not merely to praise Him for what He has done for us or given to us objectively but to speak well of what He is to us subjectively.
   B. Although the revelation in 1:3-12 is divine, it is something experienced by a human being through the Trinity of the Godhead; Peter's well speaking of the Triune God came from his experience.

Day 6 III. **We need to have the consciousness of God and the full knowledge of God (2:19; 2 Pet. 1:2, 8; 3:18):**
   A. The consciousness of God is the consciousness of one's relation to God, indicating that one is living in an intimate fellowship with God, having and keeping a good and pure conscience toward God (1 Pet. 2:19; 3:16; 1 Tim. 1:5, 19; 3:9; 2 Tim. 1:3):
      1. Our regenerated spirit has a keen sense toward God, a God-consciousness to deal with God and to sense the things of God (Rom. 1:9; 9:1).
      2. To have the consciousness of God is to live in the spirit according to God (1 Pet. 4:6; Rom. 8:2; 1 John 2:27).
   B. The full knowledge of God is an experiential knowledge of God (2 Pet. 1:2, 8):
      1. The full knowledge of the Triune God is for our participation in and enjoyment of His divine life and divine nature (vv. 3-4).
      2. In 3:18 the knowledge of the Lord is equal to the truth, the reality of all that He is; hence, to grow in the knowledge of the Lord is to grow by the realization of what Christ is, the realization of the truth (John 8:32; 17:17).

Morning Nourishment

1 Pet. Peter, an apostle of Jesus Christ, to the sojourners of
1:1-2 the dispersion,...chosen according to the foreknowledge of God the Father in the sanctification of the
Spirit unto the obedience and sprinkling of the blood
of Jesus Christ: Grace to you and peace be multiplied.
20 Who was foreknown before the foundation of the
world but has been manifested in the last of times for
your sake.

Regarding 1 Peter 1:1 and 2, we can speak of the operation, the
energetic working, of the Triune God, for here we have the Father's
choosing, the Spirit's sanctification, and the Son's redemption.
These three actions are the operation of the Triune God.

The energetic working of the Triune God is to bring us into the
enjoyment of the Triune God. To participate in God's full salvation is actually to enjoy the Triune God. When we enjoy the
Triune God, we are in grace, for grace is God for us to enjoy. It is
our enjoyment of the Triune God....Furthermore, the enjoyment
of grace results in peace [v. 2]. This means that peace results from
the enjoyment of the Triune God as grace. This is participation in the
full salvation of God, and this is the divine economy of the Trinity
of the Godhead to bring us into the participation of the Triune God.
(*Life-study of 1 Peter,* pp. 20-21)

Today's Reading

Peter begins [in 1 Peter 1:2] with God's choosing, God's selection,
in eternity. God knew us in eternity. Before we were born, before
we were created, before Adam was created, and even before the
universe was created, God foreknew us. According to God's foreknowledge, He chose us. He was like a person coming to a super-
market, looking around at all the items, and choosing the ones
that he liked. He chose each one of us in this way. It would be good
to circle the word *chosen* in our Bible. How wonderful it is that we
have been chosen according to our Father's foreknowledge!

This verse goes on to say that we were chosen in the sanctification of the Spirit. The phrase *in the sanctification of the Spirit*

functions as an adverb to modify the verb *chosen*. According to the grammar, this is one thing....We were chosen in eternity past, but we were sanctified in time. But 1 Peter 1:2 links eternity with time. In God, there is no time element. God chose us and He did it in the sanctification of the Spirit. God's choosing and the Spirit's sanctification are one action.

Then,...God's choosing us in the sanctification of the Spirit was "unto the obedience and sprinkling of the blood of Jesus Christ." (*The Spirit with Our Spirit*, pp. 88-89)

In 1:20 Peter speaks of Christ....Christ was foreordained, prepared, by God to be His redeeming Lamb (John 1:29) for His elect according to His foreknowledge before the foundation of the world. This was done according to God's eternal purpose and plan; it did not happen accidentally. Hence, in the eternal view of God, from the foundation of the world, that is, since the fall of man as a part of the world, Christ was slain (Rev. 13:8).

In 1:2 Peter speaks of the foreknowledge of God the Father, and in verse 20 he says that Christ was foreknown before the foundation of the world as the redeeming Lamb....In New Testament Greek, words such as foreknow, foreknowledge, and foreknown imply more than what we would understand from the English translations. The Greek root for these words includes the meaning of appreciation, approval, and possession....The foreknowledge of God spoken of in 1:2 implies that in eternity past God approved us and appreciated us. It also implies that in eternity past He took us over, possessed us, owned us.

For Christ to be foreknown means that He was foreordained by God. To foreknow is...to ordain beforehand....God's foreknowledge...means not only that He knew us in eternity past; it also means that He ordained us. We all were ordained by God the Father in eternity past. We do not need any other kind of ordination. (*Life-study of 1 Peter*, pp. 105-106)

Further Reading: The Spirit with Our Spirit, ch. 9; Life-study of 1 Peter, msg. 13

Enlightenment and inspiration: _____

_____

_____

_____

Morning Nourishment

1 Pet. Chosen according to the foreknowledge of God the
1:2　Father in the sanctification of the Spirit unto the obe-
　　　dience and sprinkling of the blood of Jesus Christ...
Eph.　Even as He chose us in Him before the foundation of
1:4　the world to be holy and without blemish before Him
　　　in love.
John　And when He [the Comforter] comes, He will convict
16:8　the world concerning sin and concerning righteous-
　　　ness and concerning judgment.

Concerning the sanctification of the Spirit, there are two aspects. We need to know both aspects and what they accomplish. The first aspect of sanctification precedes justification, and it carries out God's choice, His selection, and brings the chosen ones to the obedience and sprinkling of the blood for their justification. Thus, this aspect of the Spirit's sanctification is before justification through the redemption of Christ. Then, following justification, the Spirit continues to work to sanctify us dispositionally. The sequence is this: God's selection, the Spirit's sanctification, justification, and then subjective sanctification. Not many Christians have seen this....Subjective sanctification of the Spirit is revealed in Romans 6 and 15. But before we can have subjective sanctification of the Spirit, we must have the first aspect of the Spirit's sanctification, the sanctifying work that takes place before God's justification. (*Life-study of 1 Peter*, pp. 18-19)

Today's Reading

In 1 Peter 1:2 sanctification of the Spirit is not the sanctification of the Spirit which comes after justification through the redemption of Christ. Here sanctification of the Spirit is before justification through Christ's redemption (1 Cor. 6:11).

In eternity past God, according to His foreknowledge, chose us. He selected us and made a decision to gain us. But how could this selection be applied to us? In order for it to be applied, there is the need for the Spirit to separate us unto God.

Therefore, after God selected us in eternity, the Spirit came to us in time to sanctify us, to set us apart, from the world so that we would obey Christ's redemption. This means that the Spirit came to separate us for the obedience and sprinkling of the blood of Christ. It is the sanctifying Spirit who separates us from the world unto the obedience of Christ's blood. First, we repent and believe, and then we obey what Christ has done on the cross. Following this, we receive the sprinkling of the blood of Christ. This is the sanctifying work of the Spirit following God's selection to carry out God's choice and to bring us to Christ's redemption.

We all can testify of this sanctifying work of the Spirit from our experience. We were wandering on earth, perhaps never having a thought about God. Then one day the "wind" of the Spirit "blew" us to a place where we heard the preaching of the gospel. While we were listening, faith was infused into us. In this way God's selection was applied to us. In this sense the sanctification of the Spirit preceded our experience of Christ's redemption.

The Spirit separates us unto God through seeking us by enlightening us. This enlightening of the Holy Spirit is illustrated by the second parable in Luke 15, the parable of the seeking woman. Luke 15:8 says, "What woman having ten silver coins, if she loses one silver coin, does not light a lamp and sweep the house and seek carefully until she finds it?" The lamp signifies the word of God (Psa. 119:105, 130) used by the Spirit to enlighten and expose the sinner's position and condition so that he may repent. The word "sweep" indicates the searching and cleansing of the inside of a sinner. The Spirit's seeking here is inside the sinner, carried out by the Spirit's working within the repenting sinner. (*The Conclusion of the New Testament*, pp. 1285-1287)

Further Reading: Life-study of 1 Peter, msg. 2; *Living in and with the Divine Trinity,* ch. 4*

Enlightenment and inspiration: _____

_____

_____

Morning Nourishment

1 Pet. Blessed be the God and Father of our Lord Jesus
1:3 Christ, who according to His great mercy has
regenerated us unto a living hope through the
resurrection of Jesus Christ from the dead.

18-19 Knowing that *it was* not with corruptible things,
with silver or gold, *that* you were redeemed from
your vain manner of life handed down from your
fathers, but with precious blood, as of a Lamb
without blemish and without spot, *the blood* of
Christ.

23 Having been regenerated not of corruptible seed
but of incorruptible, through *the* living and abiding word of God.

The scope of Peter's ministry is wide. This is indicated by the
first two verses of 1 Peter…Here we have the Father's selection,
the Spirit's sanctification, and the Son's redemption. Of course, in
verse 2 Peter does not use the word redemption. He purposely
uses another expression—the "sprinkling of the blood of Jesus
Christ." It would have been too simple merely to use the word
redemption. But to speak of the sprinkling of the blood of Jesus
Christ is to expound the matter of redemption, define it, and
apply it. The sprinkling of the blood of Jesus Christ is the application of redemption. It is redemption expounded, defined, and
applied. (*Life-study of 1 Peter,* pp. 7-8)

Today's Reading

[First Peter 1:2] refers to the sprinkling of the blood of Jesus
Christ. In typology, the sprinkling of the atoning blood ushered
the sprinkled people into the old covenant (Exo. 24:6-8). Likewise,
the sprinkling of Christ's redeeming blood brings the sprinkled
believers into the blessing of the new covenant, that is, into the
full enjoyment of the Triune God (Heb. 9:13-14). It is a striking
mark that separates the sprinkled people from the common ones
without God. (*Life-study of 1 Peter,* p. 16)

God's choosing us in the sanctification of the Spirit was "unto the obedience and sprinkling of the blood of Jesus Christ" [1 Peter 1:2]. *Obedience* in the New Testament implies two things. First, our obedience to God implies our repentance. Then it implies our faith....These two things added together are our obedience....Following our obedience, we experience the "sprinkling of the blood of Jesus Christ." The sprinkling of the blood of Christ came upon us, not before our repentance but after our faith. God's choosing is first, and this was in the Spirit's sanctification. This resulted in obedience, consisting of repentance and faith. Then we are ready to receive God's redemption, and the first step of God's redemption is for Him to sprinkle us with His blood. Without the sprinkling, the washing, of the blood, there is no way for God to save us. (*The Spirit with Our Spirit,* p. 89)

The Father chose us in eternity past, the Holy Spirit sanctified and separated us, and Christ redeemed us by shedding His blood. Moreover, God also has regenerated us. To be regenerated means that God has put Christ into us as our life that we may have another life, the divine life, in addition to our human life. All of these basic matters—God's selection, Christ's redemption, the Holy Spirit's sanctification, the divine regeneration—are found in the writings of Peter. (*A General Sketch of the New Testament in the Light of Christ and the Church, Part 3: Hebrews through Jude,* p. 330)

First Peter 1:23 indicates that we have been regenerated through the living and abiding word of God. We have not been regenerated of corruptible seed. A seed is a container of life. The word of God as the incorruptible seed contains God's life. Hence, it is living and abiding. Through this word we have been regenerated. It is God's living and abiding word of life that conveys God's life into our spirit for our regeneration. (*Life-study of 1 Peter,* p. 120)

Further Reading: Life-study of 1 Peter, msgs. 1, 14; *A General Sketch of the New Testament in the Light of Christ and the Church, Part 3: Hebrews through Jude,* ch. 30

Enlightenment and inspiration: _____

_____

_____

_____

Morning Nourishment

1 Pet. Blessed be the God and Father of our Lord Jesus
1:3-4 Christ, who...has regenerated us unto a living hope
through the resurrection of Jesus Christ from the
dead, unto an inheritance, incorruptible and undefiled and unfading, kept in the heavens for you.
10-11 Concerning this salvation the prophets, who prophesied concerning the grace *that was to come* unto you,
sought and searched diligently, searching into what
time or what manner of time the Spirit of Christ in
them was making clear, testifying beforehand of the
sufferings of Christ and the glories after these.
Heb. ...Christ, who through the eternal Spirit offered Him-
9:14 self without blemish to God...

Eternal life is our enjoyment and also our inheritance. All the
riches of God's being are involved in His life. These riches have
become our inheritance in the heavenly bank.

In 1 Peter 1:4 Peter gives a threefold description of our inheritance. He says that this inheritance is incorruptible, undefiled,
and unfading. I believe that this threefold description points to
the Trinity. The word *incorruptible* refers to the nature of this inheritance. This is God's nature, signified by gold. *Undefiled* describes
the condition of the inheritance. This condition is related to the
sanctifying Spirit. *Unfading* refers to the expression of this inheritance. This inheritance has unfading glory....The everlasting
expression indicated by the word *unfading* is the Son as the
expression of the Father's glory. Therefore, here we have the
Father's incorruptible nature, the Spirit's sanctifying power to
maintain the inheritance in an undefiled condition, to keep it holy,
clean, and pure, and also the Son as the expression of the unfading glory. Therefore, the description of our inheritance is also a
description of the Triune God. (*Life-study of 1 Peter,* pp. 37-38)

Today's Reading

In the New Testament revelation the Spirit of Christ denotes
the Spirit after Christ's resurrection (Rom. 8:9-11). Before His

resurrection, the Spirit that is not only the Spirit of God, but the Spirit of Christ, was not yet (John 7:39). The Spirit of Christ is the Spirit of God constituted through and of the death and resurrection of Christ for the application and impartation of Christ's death and resurrection to His believers. Although the constitution of the Spirit of Christ is dispensational, constituted dispensationally through and of Christ's death and resurrection in New Testament times, His function is eternal, because He is the eternal Spirit (Heb. 9:14). This can be compared to the cross of Christ: as an event, it was accomplished at the time of Christ's death, yet its function is eternal. Hence, in the eternal sight of God, Christ was slain from the foundation of the world (Rev. 13:8). In the Old Testament time, to the prophets who were seeking out and searching out the sufferings and glories of Christ, the Spirit of God, as the Spirit of Christ, made the time and the manner of time concerning Christ's death and resurrection clear.

The important matter for us to grasp is that the constituting of the Spirit of God to become the Spirit of Christ took place after the resurrection of Christ. This means that the constituting of the Spirit of Christ is dispensational. However, the function of the Spirit of Christ is eternal, for He is the eternal Spirit.

Regarding the constitution of the Spirit of Christ, time is a factor. But regarding the function of the Spirit of Christ, time is not a factor. The Spirit of God was sufficient and adequate for creation, but for the carrying out of God's full salvation and for the application of this salvation, there is the need of the Spirit of Christ. When the Old Testament prophets were searching into what manner of time Christ would come to suffer, the Spirit of Christ was working in them. This means that the Spirit of the Triune God—the all-inclusive life-giving Spirit of Christ—was operating in them. According to function, there is no difference between the Spirit's work in the prophets and His work in the apostles. It was the same Spirit with the same function. (*Life-study of 1 Peter,* pp. 68-69, 73)

Further Reading: Life-study of 1 Peter, msgs. 4, 8-9

Enlightenment and inspiration: _____

_____

_____

_____

Morning Nourishment

1 Pet. **But according to the Holy One who called you, you**
1:15-16 **yourselves also be holy in all *your* manner of life;**
because it is written, "You shall be holy because I
am holy."

Eph. **Blessed be the God and Father of our Lord Jesus**
1:3 **Christ, who has blessed us with every spiritual**
blessing in the heavenlies in Christ.

The Holy One [in 1 Peter 1:15] is the Triune God—the choosing Father, the redeeming Son, and the sanctifying Spirit (1 Pet. 1:1-2). The Father has regenerated His elect, imparting His holy nature into them (1 Pet. 1:3); the Son has redeemed them with His blood from the vain manner of life (1 Pet. 1:18-19); and the Spirit has sanctified them according to the Father's holy nature, separating them from anything that does not fit in with God's nature so that they, by the holy nature of the Father, may become holy in all manner of life, even as holy as God Himself is.

We become holy through the sanctification of the Spirit, based on regeneration, which brings us the holy nature of God and issues in a holy life. The Father has regenerated us to produce a holy family—a holy Father with holy children. As holy children we should walk in a holy manner of life. Otherwise the Father will deal with our unholiness. He begot us with His life inwardly so that we might have His holy nature; He disciplines us outwardly so that we may partake of His holiness (Heb. 12:9-10). (*The Conclusion of the New Testament*, pp. 85-86)

Today's Reading

First Peter 1:3-12 is one long sentence. This long sentence is a blessing, a well-speaking, that involves the Trinity of the Godhead.

In 1:3 Peter uses the word *blessed*. Paul also uses this word in Ephesians 1:3: "Blessed be the God and Father of our Lord Jesus Christ, who has blessed us with every spiritual blessing in the heavenlies in Christ." In Greek the word *blessed* means well spoken of, praised with adoration. Hence, a blessing is a well-speaking, and to bless someone is to speak well of him. Therefore, to bless God is to speak well concerning Him and all that He is to us, has done for us, and will do for us. To bless God is to speak in a sweet way of what God is, of what He has done, and of what He will do. This kind of speaking is a blessing.

Many Christians think that to bless God is to praise Him. This understanding of blessing certainly is not wrong....However, in what way shall we praise God?...Many Christians praise God mainly for material things. They may say, "Oh, blessed be God the Father! Praise Him for giving me a good business, a large house, and a nice family." This falls far short of the revelation in 1 Peter 1:3-12.

Gradually the Lord has brought me into the thought of the divine revelation in the Bible. I can testify that when I read such a verse as 1:3, I realize that to bless God the Father is to speak well of what God is to us subjectively. It is not merely to praise Him for what He has done for us or given to us objectively. To bless God the Father is to speak subjectively of what He is to us, of what He has done for us, and of what He will do for us. This is to bless God according to what is revealed in the New Testament.

The source and the ground of Peter's writing are not religion or philosophy. The source and ground of Peter's writing are the experiences of the Triune God operating in him. Peter gathered together much of his experience and put the various points of his experience into writing. Peter did not care for literary style; he cared only for the genuine points of his experience of the Triune God.

Although I am short of utterance in speaking about this, I hope that this brief word will help you understand that 1:3-12 is indeed the divine revelation. This revelation is different from anything religious or philosophical. It is altogether divine. But although it is divine, it is something experienced by a human being through the Trinity of the Godhead. Therefore, Peter's well-speaking of our Triune God—the Father, the Son, and the Spirit—came from his own experience. (*Life-study of 1 Peter,* pp. 79-80, 85)

Further Reading: Life-study of 1 Peter, msgs. 10-11

Enlightenment and inspiration: _____

_____
_____
_____

Morning Nourishment

1 Pet. For this is grace, if anyone, because of a conscious-
2:19 ness of God, bears sorrows by suffering unjustly.

Rom. For God is my witness, whom I serve in my spirit in
1:9 the gospel of His Son, how unceasingly I make mention of you always in my prayers.

2 Pet. Grace to you and peace be multiplied in the full
1:2 knowledge of God and of Jesus our Lord.

3:18 But grow in the grace and knowledge of our Lord
and Savior Jesus Christ. To Him be the glory both
now and unto the day of eternity. Amen.

The consciousness of God is the consciousness of one's relation
to God, indicating that one is living in an intimate fellowship with
God, having and keeping a good and pure conscience toward God
(1 Pet. 3:16; 1 Tim. 1:5, 19; 3:9; 2 Tim. 1:3). (1 Pet. 2:19, footnote 2)

Today's Reading

Many times you want to do a certain thing. Your mind thinks
it is reasonable, and your relatives and friends all approve of it
and consider it sensible, but there is something in your deepest
part, your innermost part, that disagrees with it and says it is
wrong. There is a feeling in your deepest part; this feeling is the
feeling in your spirit, which transcends the physical feeling and
the psychological feeling. It transcends the mind and intellect,
and it transcends the soul. The feeling of the spirit is not psychological or mental, and even the more it is not physical. Rather, it is
a feeling in the deepest part of man.

The spirit was created by God for man to contact Him; hence, the
feeling of the spirit is especially keen with respect to God. The spirit
of man causes him not only to sense the need for God but also to
sense God Himself....Very often the mind and thought of man cannot perceive the things of God, yet the spirit of man can sense the
things of God....It is through the sense of the spirit that God enables
man to know Him and perceive the things that are of Him....Since
man can know God and perceive the things of God only through the
sense of the spirit, man must worship and serve God through and

in the spirit. (*The Spirit and Service in Spirit,* pp. 18-19)

In 2 Peter 1:2 we see that grace and peace also come to us in a sphere and by a particular means—the full knowledge of God and of Jesus our Lord....The full knowledge of the Triune God is for our participation in and enjoyment of His divine life and divine nature. It is not a mere doctrinal knowledge; it is an experiential knowledge, a knowledge that is full.

The Greek word rendered *full knowledge*...indicates a thorough, experiential knowledge....As we have pointed out, this is not simply a mental knowledge; it is experiential knowledge in our spiritual understanding and apprehension. The full knowledge of God and of Christ is a deep, practical, thorough, and experiential knowledge of God and our Lord. This full knowledge is both the sphere in which and the means by which the Triune God can be enjoyed by us in order that we may have a peaceful situation with Him and with all men.

[In 2 Peter 3:18] the word "grow" indicates that what Peter has written in his two Epistles is a matter of life. To grow in grace is to grow by the bountiful supply of eternal life provided by the divine power (1:3-4), and to grow in the knowledge of the Lord is to grow by the realization of what Christ is. This is to grow by the enjoyment of grace and realization of truth (John 1:14, 17).

Grace is the Triune God being life and the life supply to us. We need to grow in this life supply, in this nourishment. Therefore, to grow in grace means to grow in this inward source of the supply of life. At the beginning of this Epistle Peter speaks of grace, and now at the end he charges us to grow in this grace.

Peter also encourages us to grow in the knowledge of our Lord and Savior Jesus Christ. The realization of the knowledge of our Lord equals truth, the reality of all that He is, as in John 1:14 and 17. Peter charges the believers to grow not only in grace but also in this truth. (*Life-study of 2 Peter,* pp. 33-34, 119-120)

Further Reading: Life-study of 2 Peter, msg. 4; *The Spirit and Service in Spirit,* chs. 1, 5

Enlightenment and inspiration: _____

_____

_____

_____

Hymns, #1325

1 God eternal has a purpose,
  Formed in His eternal past,
  Spreading to eternal future;
  'Twixt these ends all time is cast.
  For with time there is the process,
  Time for His accomplishment;
  And in time we're merely travelers—
  For eternity we're meant.

2 God would have a group of people
  Built together in His plan,
  Blended, knit, coordinated
  As His vessel—one new man.
  God would come into this vessel
  With His nature, life and ways,
  Mingling Spirit with our spirits
  For His joy and to His praise.

3 God has worked in three directions
  For His plan so marvelous:
  As the Father, Son, and Spirit
  To dispense Himself to us!
  All creation gives the setting—
  Heav'n and earth are for this plan;
  'Tis for this God made a body,
  Soul and spirit—three-part man.

4 As the center, as the kernel,
  Of God's plan our spirit is;
  Calling on the name of Jesus
  Makes our spirit one with His.
  From the center to circumference
  God would saturate each part;
  Feeling, mind, and will renewing,
  Making home in all our heart.

5 Thus in life we're built together,
  Then in love we're knit as one;
  God is now His plan fulfilling,
  Finishing what He's begun.
  Lord, increase Thyself within us
  That we might be built by Thee
  Into that great corporate vessel
  Filled with God exclusively.

6   As the product, the fulfillment,
Will the church in glory stand,
Consummation of the purpose
In eternal ages planned.
God will have His corporate vessel,
All His glory to contain;
Lord, we're wholly for Thy purpose
All Thy goal in us attain.

Composition for prophecy with main point and sub-points: _____

_____
_____
_____
_____
_____
_____
_____
_____
_____
_____
_____
_____
_____
_____
_____
_____
_____
_____
_____
_____
_____
_____
_____
_____
_____
_____
_____
_____
_____
_____
_____
_____
_____

The Full Salvation of the Triune God and the Salvation of Our Souls

Scripture Reading: 1 Pet. 1:5, 9

Day 1 I. The operation of the Triune God produces the full salvation of the Triune God, composed of the Father's regeneration, the Spirit's application, and the Son's redemption (1 Pet. 1:2-3, 5, 9).

II. The full salvation of the Triune God comprises many items in three stages:

A. The first stage, the initial stage, is the stage of regeneration:

   1. This stage is composed of redemption, sanctification (positional—v. 2; 1 Cor. 6:11), justification, reconciliation, and regeneration.

   2. In this stage God justified us through the redemption of Christ (Rom. 3:24-26) and regenerated us in our spirit with His life by His Spirit (John 3:3-6); thus we received God's eternal salvation (Heb. 5:9) and His eternal life (John 3:15) and became His children (1:12-13), who shall not perish forever (10:28-29).

   3. This initial salvation has saved us from God's condemnation and from eternal perdition (3:18, 16).

Day 2 B. The second stage, the progressing stage, is the stage of transformation:

   1. This stage is composed of freedom from sin, sanctification (mainly dispositional—Rom. 6:19, 22), growth in life, transformation, building up, and maturing.

   2. In this stage God is freeing us from the dominion of indwelling sin—the law of sin and of death—by the law of the Spirit of life, through the subjective working of the

effectiveness of the death of Christ in us (vv. 6-7; 7:16-20; 8:2); sanctifying us by His Holy Spirit (15:16) with His holy nature, through His discipline (Heb. 12:10) and His judgment in His own house (1 Pet. 4:17); causing us to grow in His life (1 Cor. 3:6-7); transforming us by renewing the inward parts of our soul by the life-giving Spirit (2 Cor. 3:6, 17-18; Rom. 12:2; Eph. 4:23) through the working of all things (Rom. 8:28); building us together into a spiritual house for His dwelling (1 Pet. 2:5; Eph. 2:22); and maturing us in His life (Rev. 14:15) for the completion of His full salvation.

3. In this way we are being delivered from the power of sin, the world, the flesh, self, the soul (the natural life), and individualism into maturity in the divine life for the fulfillment of God's eternal purpose.

Day 3   C. The third stage, the completing stage, is the stage of glorification:

1. This stage is composed of the redemption (transfiguration) of our body, conformity to the Lord, glorification, the inheritance of God's kingdom, participation in Christ's kingship, and the topmost enjoyment of the Lord.

2. In this stage God will redeem our fallen and corrupted body (Rom. 8:23) by transfiguring it into the body of Christ's glory (Phil. 3:21); conform us to the glorious image of His firstborn Son (Rom. 8:29), making us wholly and absolutely like Him in our regenerated spirit, transformed soul, and transfigured body; and glorify us (v. 30), immersing us in His glory (Heb. 2:10) that we may enter into His heavenly kingdom (2 Tim. 4:18; 2 Pet. 1:11), into which He has called us (1 Thes. 2:12), and inherit it as the topmost portion of His blessing (James 2:5;

Gal. 5:21)—even that we may reign with Christ as His co-kings, participating in His kingship over the nations (2 Tim. 2:12; Rev. 20:4, 6; 2:26-27; 12:5) and sharing His royal, kingly joy in His divine government (Matt. 25:21, 23).

3. In this way our body will be freed from the slavery of corruption of the old creation into the freedom of the glory of God's new creation (Rom. 8:21), and our soul will be delivered out of the realm of trials and sufferings into a new realm, one that is full of glory, and will share in and enjoy all that the Triune God is, has, and has accomplished, attained, and obtained (1 Pet. 1:6; 3:14; 4:12-13; 5:9-10).

Day 4 III. The salvation in 1:5 is full salvation, ultimate salvation; it refers specifically to the salvation of our souls from the dispensational punishment of the Lord's governmental dealing at His coming back:

Losing of our renewed (soul life)

A. This is the salvation—the salvation of our souls—which is ready to be revealed to us at the last time, the grace to be brought to us at the revelation of Christ in glory; the salvation of our souls is the end of our faith (vv. 9, 13; Matt. 16:27).

B. Our soul will be saved from sufferings into the full enjoyment of the Lord at His revelation, His coming back (25:31):

1. For this salvation we must deny our soul, our soulish life, with all its pleasures in this age so that we may gain it in the enjoyment of the Lord in the coming age (10:37-39; 16:24-27; Luke 17:30-33; John 12:25):

Day 5

a. To lose the soul-life means to lose the enjoyment of the soul, and to save the soul-life means to preserve the soul in its enjoyment (Matt. 16:25).

b. We will either lose our soul-life today and

gain it in the coming age, or save our soul-
life today and lose it in the coming age.

c. If we would enter into the Lord's joy in the
coming age, we need to pay the price in
this age by losing our soul-life (25:21, 23).

2. At the Lord's revelation, through His judgment seat, some believers will enter into
the joy of the Lord, and some will suffer in
weeping and gnashing of teeth (vv. 21, 23;
24:45-46; 25:30; 24:51).

Day 6

3. To enter into the Lord's joy is the salvation
of our souls (Heb. 10:39):

a. The saving, or gaining, of our soul depends
on how we deal with our soul in following
the Lord after we are saved and regenerated.

b. If we lose our soul now for the Lord's
sake, we will save it, and it will be saved,
or gained, at the Lord's coming back
(Luke 9:24; 1 Pet. 1:9).

c. The gaining of the soul will be the
reward of the kingdom to the overcoming
followers of the Lord (Heb. 10:35; Matt.
16:22-28).

C. The power of God is able to guard us unto this
salvation so that we may obtain it; the power of
God is the cause of our being guarded, and faith
is the means through which the power of God
becomes effective in guarding us (1 Pet. 1:5).

D. We should eagerly expect this marvelous, full,
and ultimate salvation and prepare ourselves
for its splendid revelation (Rom. 8:19, 23).

Morning Nourishment

1 Pet. **Blessed be the God and Father of our Lord Jesus**
1:3 **Christ, who according to His great mercy has regen-**
erated us unto a living hope through the resurrec-
tion of Jesus Christ from the dead.
5 **Who are being guarded by the power of God through**
faith unto a salvation ready to be revealed at the
last time.
John **For God so loved the world that He gave His only**
3:16 **begotten Son, that everyone who believes into Him**
would not perish, but would have eternal life.

In 1 Peter 1:1 and 2, we have the operation of the Triune God:
the selection of God the Father, the sanctification of the Spirit,
and the sprinkling of the blood of Jesus Christ. Then in the
remainder of the first chapter we have the full salvation of the
Triune God. This full salvation is composed of the Father's regeneration, the Spirit's application, and the Son's redemption. The
Father's regeneration has brought His eternal life into us and has
also brought us into the enjoyment of this eternal life. Now this
enjoyment is a living hope for us today. (*Life-study of 1 Peter,* p. 52)

Today's Reading

The word "salvation" in 1 Peter 1:5 denotes the full salvation of
the Triune God....It does not refer only to a part of our salvation,
to that initial aspect of salvation that comes through the Savior,
Jesus Christ. Rather, this is the full salvation of the Triune God, of
the Father, the Son, and the Spirit. In this full salvation a great
part is accomplished by the Father; another great part, by the
Son; and yet another great part, by the Spirit. Therefore, this salvation is the full salvation of the Trinity of the Godhead.

The full salvation of the Triune God comprises many items in
three stages:...the initial stage, the progressing stage, and the
completing stage. These three stages are not divided according to
knowledge or merely according to objective aspects of God's salvation. On the contrary, these stages are arranged according to life.
Spiritual life, as we all know, begins with regeneration, continues

in transformation, and reaches maturity in the stage of consummation. Therefore, these three stages of salvation are divided according to the experience of life.

The initial stage, the stage of regeneration, is composed of redemption, sanctification (positional—1:2; 1 Cor. 6:11), justification, reconciliation, and regeneration....Regeneration is the totality of redemption, sanctification, justification, and reconciliation. Regeneration is the result of these four matters.

In the stage of regeneration God has justified us through the redemption of Christ (Rom. 3:24-26), and He has regenerated us in our spirit with His life by His Spirit (John 3:3-6). Thus, we have received God's eternal salvation (Heb. 5:9) and His eternal life (John 3:15), and we have become His children (John 1:12-13), who shall not perish forever (John 10:28-29).

God has regenerated us in our spirit. The element, the substance, God used to regenerate us is His own life. Furthermore, this regeneration with God's life was accomplished by a person, that is, by God's Spirit. As a result of this regeneration,...we have already received God's salvation. No one can deny that we have received God's salvation in its first stage. There is no need for us to grow unto this stage, and it is not necessary for us to wait until it is revealed to us. We have received two things that are eternal—eternal salvation and eternal life. This...is the revelation of God's pure Word.

Because we have been regenerated and have received God's eternal salvation and eternal life, we have become God's children. As children of God, we shall never perish. This truth should strengthen us and keep us from the erroneous teaching that says if we sin after we have been saved, we shall perish. That teaching is nonsensical and is absolutely not according to the truth. Once we have received God's eternal salvation, we are saved forever, for eternity. God's eternal salvation is not dispensational; it is not temporary. Because it is an eternal salvation, we shall never perish. (*Life-study of 1 Peter,* pp. 56-58)

Further Reading: Life-study of 1 Peter, msgs. 5-6

Enlightenment and inspiration: _____

_____

_____

_____

Morning Nourishment

Rom. **But now, having been freed from sin and enslaved**
6:22 **to God, you have your fruit unto sanctification,**
     and the end, eternal life.
8:2 **For the law of the Spirit of life has freed me in**
     Christ Jesus from the law of sin and of death.
12:2 **And do not be fashioned according to this age, but**
     be transformed by the renewing of the mind that
     you may prove what the will of God is, that which
     is good and well pleasing and perfect.

Salvation is not a simple matter. Salvation covers a long span and cannot be enjoyed or experienced all at once. God's full salvation is of three stages: the initial stage, the progressing stage, and the completing stage. I would encourage all the saints, especially the young people, to gain a thorough knowledge of these three stages of God's full salvation. In particular, we need to understand what God's salvation does for us in each stage. We need to know from what we are delivered by each stage of God's full salvation. We also need to know the items or aspects of this salvation and its results. In each of the three stages of God's full salvation we are delivered from particular things, we experience certain matters, and we have definite results. (*Life-study of 1 Peter*, p. 56)

Today's Reading

[The] initial salvation of God has saved us from God's condemnation and from eternal perdition (John 3:18, 16). However,...it does not save us from God's discipline. During our lifetime God will discipline us and may even punish us....This does not mean, however, that those who are disciplined by God will lose their salvation. According to the Scriptures, on the one hand, we have been saved for eternity. We shall never be condemned by God, and we shall never perish. On the other hand, while we are living on earth in the flesh, God will deal with us and discipline us. Sometimes He may even judge us or punish us....Through the initial stage of God's salvation,...God may punish us for certain things, but we have been saved for eternity and we shall never lose this eternal salvation.

The second stage of God's full salvation, the progressing stage, is the stage of transformation. This stage is composed of freedom from sin, sanctification (mainly dispositional—Rom. 6:19, 22), growth in life, transformation, building up, and maturing. The sanctification in this stage is mainly dispositional, although there is still an amount of positional sanctification. In the first stage sanctification is altogether positional; in the second stage sanctification is mainly dispositional.

In this stage of transformation God is freeing us from the dominion of indwelling sin—the law of sin and death—by the law of the Spirit of life through the effectiveness of the death of Christ working subjectively in us (Rom. 6:6-7; 7:16-20; 8:2). In the second stage God is also sanctifying us by His Holy Spirit (Rom. 15:16), with His holy nature, through His discipline (Heb. 12:10) and His judgment in His own house (1 Pet. 4:17). God is now sanctifying us by a person, and this person is the Holy Spirit. The element, the substance, God uses to sanctify us is His holy nature. The means through which we are sanctified is God's discipline and judgment, the judgment He exercises in governing His own house.

In the progressing stage of salvation God is also causing us to grow in His life (1 Cor. 3:6-7). He is transforming us by renewing the inward parts of our soul by the life-giving Spirit (2 Cor. 3:6, 17-18; Rom. 12:2; Eph. 4:23) through the working of all things (Rom. 8:28). He is building us together into a spiritual house for His dwelling (1 Pet. 2:5; Eph. 2:22), and He is maturing us in His life (Rev. 14:15) for the completion of His full salvation.

In the first stage of God's salvation we are saved from God's condemnation and from eternal perdition. But in the second stage we are being delivered from the power of sin, the world, the flesh, the self, the soul (the natural life), and individualism,...that we would have maturity in the divine life for the fulfilling of God's eternal purpose. (*Life-study of 1 Peter*, pp. 58-59)

Further Reading: Life-study of 1 Peter, msg. 7; *God's New Testament Economy*, chs. 11-13

Enlightenment and inspiration: _____

_____

_____

_____

Morning Nourishment

Rom. ...We ourselves,...who have the firstfruits of the Spirit,
8:23 even we ourselves groan in ourselves, eagerly awaiting sonship, the redemption of our body.
Phil. Who will transfigure the body of our humiliation to
3:21 be conformed to the body of His glory, according to
His operation by which He is able even to subject all
things to Himself.
1 Thes. So that you might walk in a manner worthy of God,
2:12 who calls you into His own kingdom and glory.

The third stage of God's full salvation, the completing stage, is
the stage of consummation. This stage is composed of the redemption (transfiguration) of our body, conformity to the Lord, glorification, inheritance of God's kingdom, participation in Christ's
kingship, and the topmost enjoyment of the Lord. These matters
are beyond our present experience. They will be revealed to us in
the future. Although we have experienced the first stage of salvation and are now in the second stage, the third stage is still far
beyond us. The items in this stage will be revealed at the unveiling of the Lord Jesus. (*Life-study of 1 Peter,* pp. 59-60)

Today's Reading

In the completing stage of salvation, God will redeem our
fallen and corrupted body (Rom. 8:23) by transfiguring it into
the body of Christ's glory (Phil. 3:21). He will conform us to the
glorious image of His firstborn Son (Rom. 8:29), making us holy
and absolutely like Him in our regenerated spirit, transformed
soul, and transfigured body. He will also glorify us (Rom. 8:30),
immersing us in His glory (Heb. 2:10) that we may enter into His
heavenly kingdom (2 Tim. 4:18; 2 Pet. 1:11), into which He has
called us (1 Thes. 2:12), and inherit it as the topmost portion of His
blessing (James 2:5; Gal. 5:21), even to reign with Christ, to be His
co-kings, participating in His kingship over the nations (2 Tim.
2:12; Rev. 20:4, 6; 2:26-27; 12:5) and sharing His royal, kingly joy
in His divine government (Matt. 25:21, 23). Our body will be freed
from the slavery of corruption of the old creation into the freedom

of the glory of God's new creation (Rom. 8:21), and our soul will be delivered out of the realm of trials and sufferings (1 Pet. 1:6; 4:12; 3:14; 5:9) into a new realm, full of glory (4:13; 5:10). In this new realm we shall share and enjoy all the Triune God is, has, and has accomplished, attained, and obtained.

In this country we may suffer in one way, whereas those in other countries may suffer in a different way. Wherever we may be, we shall suffer and be subject to God's discipline. There is no way for us to avoid suffering in our soul. To live on earth as a human being is to suffer. The earth today is not for our enjoyment.

The young people may expect to finish their education, find a good job, and then have a very pleasant married life. They need to realize, however, that on this earth there is no paradise. We must wait for the Lord's coming to be saved from the realm of suffering into a realm of comfort. That will be the full salvation of our soul.

I can testify that although I have a good wife and although I am loved by the saints and the churches, I continue to suffer a great deal in my soul. No one can help me to avoid this suffering. Therefore, I am waiting for the unveiling of the Lord Jesus. At the time of His coming back, I shall be rescued from this realm of suffering into a realm of enjoyment. In that realm we shall have the full enjoyment of the Triune God and of all that He is, has, and has accomplished, attained, and obtained.

This is the salvation of our souls that is ready to be revealed to us at the last time. This is also the grace that will be brought to us at the unveiling of Christ in glory (1:13; Matt. 16:27; 25:31). Furthermore, this is the end of our faith (1 Pet. 1:9). The power of God is able to guard us unto this that we may obtain it. Therefore, we should eagerly expect such a marvelous salvation (Rom. 8:23), and we should prepare ourselves for its splendid revelation (Rom. 8:19). Hallelujah for the full salvation of the Triune God in its three stages! (*Life-study of 1 Peter,* pp. 60-61)

Further Reading: Life-study of 1 Peter, msg. 8; *The Basic Revelation in the Holy Scriptures,* chs. 1-4

Enlightenment and inspiration: _____

_____

_____

Morning Nourishment

1 Pet. Receiving the end of your faith, the salvation of your
1:9 souls.
   13 Therefore girding up the loins of your mind *and* being
      sober, set your hope perfectly on the grace being
      brought to you at the revelation of Jesus Christ.
John He who loves his soul-life loses it; and he who hates his
12:25 soul-life in this world shall keep it unto eternal life.

According to 1 Peter 1:5, we are being guarded, garrisoned (a
military term), by the power of God through faith unto salvation.
The result of this guarding is salvation.

The salvation spoken of in verse 5 is full salvation, ultimate
salvation. Specifically, it refers not to salvation from eternal
perdition, but refers to the salvation of our souls from the dispensational punishment of the Lord's governmental dealing. This
dispensational punishment of God's governmental dealing is
neglected by most Christians today. They seem to have no light
concerning it nor understanding of it. Although such a revelation
is found in the Bible, most Christians do not have it in their
concept. (*Life-study of 1 Peter,* pp. 39-40)

Today's Reading

Even though we are saved, we need to ask ourselves:...If the
Lord Jesus were to come back today, would you be ready to appear
before His judgment seat? Could you stand before Him there in
peace? No doubt, your conscience would tell you that in many
things you have not yet been saved. If this is your situation, then
the judgment at the judgment seat of Christ may have a negative
result as far as you are concerned. However, I hope that the result
for us all will be positive. But should the result be negative, we
shall experience some kind of punishment. That will not be eternal perdition; rather, it will be the dispensational punishment of
God's governmental dealing.

[First Peter 1:7 speaks of "the proving of your faith." Verse 9] is
the direct continuation of verse 7. The proving of our faith to be
found unto praise, glory, and honor results in the obtaining of the

end of our faith, that is, the salvation of our souls.

The salvation in verse 9 is full salvation, the salvation which is in three stages—the initial stage, the progressing stage, and the completing stage. We are of three parts: spirit, soul, and body. Our spirit has been saved through regeneration (John 3:5-6). Our body will be saved, redeemed, through the coming transfiguration (Rom. 8:23; Phil. 3:21). Our soul will be saved from sufferings into the full enjoyment of the Lord at His unveiling, His coming back. For this we have to deny our soul, our soulish life, with all its pleasures in this age, that we may gain it in the enjoyment of the Lord in the coming age (Matt. 10:37-39; 16:24-27; Luke 17:30-33; John 12:25). At the Lord's unveiling some believers, through His judgment seat, will enter into the joy of the Lord (Matt. 25:21, 23; 24:45-46), and some will suffer in weeping and gnashing of teeth (Matt. 25:30; 24:51). To enter into the Lord's joy is the salvation of our souls (Heb. 10:39). (*Life-study of 1 Peter,* pp. 40, 50)

If today we love only the Lord and not our soul, that is, our self, and if we live by Him and according to His standard, then when He comes back He will reward us with the kingdom....However, if we are defeated believers, we shall be punished during the kingdom age, and that punishment will involve our soul, with the gnashing of teeth as a sign of suffering in our soul.

Today many believers are loose or indifferent in following the Lord mainly because they love their soul. They want such things as greatness and prosperity for the enjoyment of the soul. To allow the soul to have its enjoyment in this age is to save the soul. But to suffer in our soul because of following the Lord is to lose our soul. If we lose our soul today, willing to suffer and be dishonored for the Lord's name, we shall gain our soul and save our soul when the Lord comes back. When we are rewarded by Him, our soul will be saved and gained, and we shall enjoy the salvation of the soul. (*The Conclusion of the New Testament,* pp. 2016-2017)

Further Reading: The Conclusion of the New Testament, msg. 186; *The Collected Works of Watchman Nee,* vol. 17, pp. 19-53

Enlightenment and inspiration: _____

_____

_____

_____

Morning Nourishment

Matt. ...Whoever wants to save his soul-life shall lose it; but
16:25 whoever loses his soul-life for My sake shall find it.
25:21 His master said to him, Well *done,* good and faithful
slave. You were faithful over a few things; I will set you
over many things. Enter into the joy of your master.
2 Pet. For in this way the entrance into the eternal kingdom
1:11 of our Lord and Savior Jesus Christ will be richly *and*
bountifully supplied to you.

According to the context of Matthew 16, the self in verse 24 is
the embodiment and expression of the soul in verse 25....In verse
25 the word soul indicates enjoyment. If you consider the context
of verses 25 through 27, you will see that the Lord is speaking
about the enjoyment of the soul. To save the soul is to allow the
soul to have its enjoyment. Thus, the self is the expression of the
soul, and the soul itself is the enjoyment. To lose the soul means to
lose the enjoyment of the soul, and to gain the soul means to have
the enjoyment of the soul. (*The Exercise of the Kingdom for the
Building of the Church,* pp. 44-45)

Today's Reading

God's intention in His creation of man was that man would
take Him in and express Him. Taking in God and expressing God
should be man's joy and amusement. Man's happiness and entertainment must be God Himself, and this is not an objective God,
but a subjective God. To take God in and to live God out is man's joy.
We should not blame people for desiring amusement, for God created man with the need for enjoyment....Because people have lost
God, they seek entertainment by going to the movies, theater, and
various sporting events. They have not found the fulfillment of
their need for entertainment in God Himself. God Himself is the
unique fulfillment of our need for entertainment....All the amuse-
ments people seek outside of God are for the satisfaction of the soul.

If man had expressed God on earth, God would have been able
to recover the earth. Then both man and God would have enjoyed
the earth. God would have been happy, and we would have been

happy also. However, man did not cooperate with God. Thus, God did not have a way to recover the earth. Rather, He Himself has even been rejected by the earth. When He came in the flesh, He was rejected. This present age, the age of the church, is the age of the world's rejection of Christ. Because Christ has been rejected, at present He has no joy on this earth. As His followers, we share His destiny. Our destiny as followers of the Lord Jesus is not to be welcomed by this world; instead, it is to be rejected. Therefore, this age is not the time for us to have enjoyment for our soul; it is the time for us to lose this enjoyment. When the Lord Jesus comes back, that will be the time for Him to enjoy the earth. Satan will be bound, Christ will recover the earth, and the entire earth will be under His reign. At that time Christ will enjoy the earth, and all His followers will participate in this enjoyment....This will be the saving of our soul. In order to have the enjoyment in the coming age, we need to pay the price in this age by losing our soul.

[Second Peter 1:11 speaks of an entrance into the eternal kingdom being richly and bountifully supplied to us.] We all need a rich entrance into the eternal kingdom of the Lord. We can have such an entrance by losing our souls today. The more we lose the enjoyment of the soul, the richer an entrance we shall have.

We have seen that although we have been saved in our spirit, we still need the salvation of our soul. Now is the time for us to lose our soul that we may gain it at the Lord's coming back. We need to lose everything that makes our soul happy. By losing our soul, our entire being will be daily and gradually transformed. Then we shall have the position to be rewarded with the saving of the soul in the future. Outwardly we shall save our soul at the Lord's coming, and inwardly we shall be qualified to participate in the Lord's enjoyment in the coming age. (*The Exercise of the Kingdom for the Building of the Church*, pp. 58-59, 63)

Further Reading: The Exercise of the Kingdom for the Building of the Church, ch. 5; Life-study of Matthew, msg. 48; Life-study of Luke, msg. 33

Enlightenment and inspiration: _____

_____

_____

_____

Morning Nourishment

Luke For whoever wants to save his soul-life shall lose it;
9:24-25 but whoever loses his soul-life for My sake, this one
shall save it. For what is a man profited if he gains
the whole world but loses or forfeits himself?
Heb. But we are not of those who shrink back to ruin but
10:39 of them who have faith to the gaining of the soul.

First Peter 1:5 and Hebrews 10:39 are also related to the
saving of the soul. The salvation in 1 Peter 1:5 is not salvation
from eternal perdition, but salvation of our souls from the
dispensational punishment of the Lord's governmental dealing.
Hebrews 10:39 speaks of the gaining of the soul. At the time we
believed in the Lord Jesus and were saved, our spirit was regenerated with the Spirit of God (John 3:6). But we must wait until
the Lord Jesus comes back for our body to be redeemed, saved,
and transfigured (Rom. 8:23-25; Phil. 3:21). As to the saving, or
gaining, of our soul, it depends upon how we deal with it in following the Lord after we are saved and regenerated. If we would lose
it now for the Lord's sake, we shall save it (Matt. 16:25; Luke 9:24;
17:33; John 12:25; 1 Pet. 1:9), and it will be saved, or gained, at the
Lord's coming back. This will be a reward to the overcoming followers of the Lord (Matt. 16:22-28). (*Life-study of James,* p. 109)

Today's Reading

Not many Christians have a clear understanding of the salvation of the soul or of the verses that refer to this matter (Matt.
16:25; Heb. 10:39; James 1:21). When I was young, I was troubled
by these verses. I said to myself, "I have received salvation
already. Why must I wait to receive the salvation of the soul?"
According to the New Testament, we all have received salvation
in our spirit. When we believed in the Lord Jesus and were
washed in His blood, we were regenerated by the Holy Spirit and
saved. Although the salvation in our spirit is ours already, there is
another kind of salvation, the salvation of our soul, for which we
must wait until the Lord comes back.

Our spirit has been saved in this age, and we cannot lose this salvation. But it is not yet determined whether or not our soul will be saved at the Lord's coming. Unlike the salvation of the spirit, the salvation of the soul is not a matter of simple faith. By confessing our sins, believing in the Lord Jesus, and calling on His name, we are regenerated and have salvation in our spirit. But the salvation of the soul requires a long process.

Throughout the world there is the enjoyment of the soul. The reason people study to earn a degree is to have a better life, and a better life means more enjoyment. Others work to earn a promotion in their job that they may have more money for more enjoyment of the soul. When the Lord Jesus came, He lost His soul, that is, He gave up all His soulish enjoyment. He lost the enjoyment of His soul in this age so that He might gain His soul in the coming age. As we have seen, in the coming age the Lord Jesus will enjoy the whole earth. At that time He will invite us, His partners, to share in this enjoyment. We need to wait patiently for the coming enjoyment. If you keep the enjoyment in your soul today, you will lose the enjoyment to come....The choice is yours. If you prefer to have your enjoyment today, you are free to do so. But if you save your soul in this age, be assured that you will lose it when the Lord comes back. He will tell you that because you have enjoyed your soul so much, now is the time for you to lose it. Which do you choose—to lose your soul today and gain it tomorrow, or to gain it today and lose it tomorrow? If we could gain the whole world, it would still not be worthwhile to gain it at the cost of losing our soul. (*The Exercise of the Kingdom for the Building of the Church,* pp. 53-54, 57-58, 60)

This is the end of our faith, [the salvation of our souls]. The power of God is able to guard us unto this that we may obtain it (1 Pet. 1:9). We should eagerly expect such a marvelous salvation (Rom. 8:23) and prepare ourselves for its splendid revelation (v. 19). (*Life-study of 1 Peter,* p. 42)

Further Reading: The Exercise of the Kingdom for the Building of the Church, chs. 6-7

Enlightenment and inspiration: _____

_____

_____

_____

Hymns, #887

1 The name of Jesus is our stand,
   It is our victory;
  Not on ourselves do we rely,
   But, mighty Lord, on Thee.
  Our weapons are not arms of flesh,
   But ours the Spirit's sword,
  And God's whole armor putting on,
   We battle in the Lord.

2 Behold, the foe doth meet and plot,
   Stand firm in one accord!
  Though war be fierce and darkness thick,
   Resist him in the Lord!
  If one thru fear should backward turn,
   He undermines the rest.
  Oh, do not let your brothers down,
   Nor by you be distressed.

3 The devil knows his time is short,
   He is the more enraged,
  And by his wiles would weaken us
   Before the battle's waged.
  The trials now more numerous are,
   The suff'ring e'en more sore,
  The force of hell opposing us
   More dreadful than before.

4 What should our posture be today
   In such a desperate hour?
  Should we our ease and pleasure seek
   And let the foe devour?
  Or with increasing conflict strong,
   Courageous to endure?
  'Tis here that life or death is won!
   Who will God's praise secure?

5 For Christ the Lord we then would stand,
   He is the Conqueror!
  For Him we would endure the pain
   Until the fight is o'er.
  The hour of triumph soon we'll see—
   The Lord will come again;
  If now we suffer for His sake,
   Then we with Him shall reign.

Composition for prophecy with main point and sub-points: Choices.

Lose soul life 🗲 Gain God

Love God 🗲 Hate world

Joy 🗲 Suffer

Life and Building in 1 and 2 Peter

Scripture Reading: 1 Pet. 1:8; 2:1-5, 9; 2 Pet. 1:3-4

Day 1   I. **The central thought of Peter's Epistles and of the entire Scriptures is life and building (1 Pet. 1:23; 2:2-5; 2 Pet. 1:3-4):**

A. Life is the Triune God embodied in Christ and realized as the Spirit dispensing Himself into us for our enjoyment, and building is the church, the Body of Christ, God's spiritual house, as the enlargement and expansion of God for the corporate expression of God (Gen. 2:8-9, 22; Matt. 16:18; Col. 2:19; Eph. 4:16).

B. Christ, as the seed of life, is the power of life within us that has granted to us all things which relate to life and godliness for the building up of the church as the rich surplus of life and the expression of life through the growth and development of life (2 Pet. 1:3-4; cf. Acts 3:15; *Hymns,* #203, stanza 4).

Day 2 II. **God's goal is to have a spiritual house built up with living stones (1 Pet. 2:5):**

A. As life to us, Christ is the incorruptible seed; for God's building, He is the living stone (1:23; 2:4).

B. At Peter's conversion the Lord gave him a new name, Peter—a stone (John 1:42); and when Peter received the revelation concerning Christ, the Lord revealed further that He was the rock—a stone (Matt. 16:16-18); by these two incidents Peter received the impression that both Christ and His believers are living stones for God's building (1 Pet. 2:4-8; Acts 4:10-12; Isa. 28:16; Zech. 4:7).

C. We, the believers in Christ, are living stones as the duplication of Christ through regeneration and transformation; we were created of clay (Rom. 9:21), but at regeneration we received the seed of the divine life, which by its growing in us transforms us into living stones (1 Pet. 2:5).

Day 3 **III. Since God's building is living, it is growing;
the actual building up of the church as the
house of God is by the believers' growth in
life (Eph. 2:21):**

A. In order to grow in life for God's building, we
must love the Lord, take heed to our spirit, and
guard our heart with all vigilance to stay on the
pathway of life (1 Pet. 1:8; 2:2, 5; 3:4, 15; Prov.
4:18-23; Deut. 10:12; Mark 12:30).

B. If we want Christ's life to be unhindered in us, we
must experience the breaking of the cross, the
killing death of Christ in the all-inclusive Spirit
of Christ as the Spirit of glory, so that the following obstacles within us can be dealt with and
removed (1 Pet. 1:11; 4:14; Psa. 139:23-24):

1. Being a Christian means not taking anything
other than Christ as our aim; the obstacle to
this is not knowing the pathway of life and
not taking Christ as our life (Matt. 7:13-14;
Phil. 3:8-14; Col. 3:4; Rom. 8:28-29).

2. The second obstacle is hypocrisy; a person's
spirituality is not determined by outward
appearance but by how he takes care of
Christ (Matt. 6:1-6; 15:7-8; John 5:44;
12:42-43; cf. Josh. 7:21).

3. The third obstacle is rebellion; we may be
very active and zealous in doing things but
still imprison and disobey the living Christ
within us by ignoring Him (Lev. 14:9, 14-18;
11:1-2, 46-47; Rom. 16:17; 1 Cor. 15:33).

Day 4 4. The fourth obstacle is our natural capabilities; if our natural capabilities remain unbroken in us, they will become a problem to
Christ's life (2:14-15; 3:12, 16-17; Jude 19;
cf. Lev. 10:1-2).

C. In order to grow in life for God's building, we
must put away "all malice and all guile and
hypocrisies and envyings and all evil speakings"
(1 Pet. 2:1).

Day 5

    D. In order to grow in life for God's building, we must be nourished with the guileless milk of God's word (v. 2):

      1. The guileless milk is conveyed in the word of God to nourish our inner man through the understanding of our rational mind and is assimilated by our mental faculties (Rom. 8:6; cf. Deut. 11:18).

      2. Although the nourishing milk of the word is for the soul through the mind, it eventually nourishes the spirit, making us not soulish but spiritual, suitable for being built up as a spiritual house of God (cf. 1 Cor. 2:15).

      3. In order to enjoy the milk of the word, to taste God with His goodness in the word, we must receive His word by means of all prayer and muse on His word (1 Pet. 2:3; Eph. 6:17-18; Psa. 119:15, 23, 48, 78, 99, 148):

        a. To muse on the word is to taste and enjoy it through careful considering (1 Pet. 2:2-3; Psa. 119:103).

        b. Prayer, speaking to oneself, and praising the Lord may also be included in musing on the word; to muse on the word is to "chew the cud," to receive the word of God through much reconsideration (Lev. 11:3).

      4. By feeding on Christ as the nourishing milk in the word, we grow unto full salvation, unto maturity through transformation for glorification; salvation in 1 Peter 2:2 is a matter of transformation for God's building.

      5. We enjoy the "milk-Christ" to nourish us so that we may be transformed with Him as the "stone-Christ" and be built up as the "Body-Christ," as God's spiritual house into a holy priesthood (vv. 2-5; 1 Cor. 12:12-13).

Day 6   **IV. The holy priesthood, the coordinated body of priests, is the built-up spiritual house; God wants a spiritual house for His dwelling and** a priestly body, a corporate priesthood, for His service (1 Pet. 2:5; Exo. 19:5-6):

A. We are "a chosen race, a royal priesthood, a holy nation, a people acquired for a possession" (1 Pet. 2:9)—*chosen race* denotes our descent from God; *royal priesthood,* our service to God; *holy nation,* our being a community for God; and *people acquired for a possession,* our preciousness to God.

B. Our corporate priestly service is to tell out as the gospel the virtues of the One who has called us out of darkness into His marvelous light (v. 9) so that we may "offer up spiritual sacrifices acceptable to God through Jesus Christ" (v. 5b); these spiritual sacrifices are:

1. Christ as the reality of all the sacrifices of the Old Testament types, such as the burnt offering, meal offering, peace offering, sin offering, and trespass offering (Lev. 1—5).

2. The sinners saved by our gospel preaching, offered as members of Christ (Rom. 15:16).

3. Our body, our praises, and the things that we do for God (12:1; Heb. 13:15-16; Phil. 4:18).

C. All our priestly service to the Lord must originate from Him as "the God of measure" and not from ourselves; all our priestly service must be according to His leading and His limitation, as we allow His death to operate in us, so that His resurrection life can be imparted through us into others (2 Cor. 10:13; John 12:24; 21:15-22; 2 Sam. 7:18, 25, 27; Luke 1:37-38; *Hymns,* #907).

Morning Nourishment

Matt. ...He spoke many things to them in parables, saying,
13:3 Behold, the sower went out to sow.
1 Cor. I planted, Apollos watered, but God caused the growth.
3:6-7, 9 So then neither is he who plants anything nor he
who waters, but God who causes the growth....For
we are God's fellow workers; you are God's cultivated land, God's building.
1 Pet. Coming to Him, a living stone, rejected by men but
2:4-5 with God chosen *and* precious, you yourselves also,
as living stones, are being built up as a spiritual
house into a holy priesthood to offer up spiritual
sacrifices acceptable to God through Jesus Christ.

[Christ is the living stone in 1 Peter 2:4.] A living stone is one
that not only possesses life, but also grows in life. This is Christ for
God's building. Here Peter changes his metaphor from the seed of
the vegetable life (1:23-24) to the stone of minerals. The seed is for
life-planting; the stone is for building (2:5). Peter's thought has gone
on from life-planting to God's building. As life to us, Christ is the
seed. For God's building, He is the stone. After receiving Him as
the seed of life, we need to grow that we may experience Him as the
stone living in us. Thus He will make us also living stones, transformed with His stone nature so that we may be built together
with others a spiritual house upon Him as both the foundation and
the cornerstone (Isa. 28:16). (*Life-study of 1 Peter,* pp. 136-137)

Today's Reading

Ephesians 4:15 and 16 say, "But holding to truth in love, we
may grow up into Him in all things, who is the Head, Christ, out
from whom all the Body...causes the growth of the Body unto the
building up of itself in love." In these two verses we clearly see
growth and building together. One is the cause, and the other is
the effect; there is growth, and then there is the building. We need
to learn how to grow and how to help others to grow.

God's intention is to put Christ as the seed of life into us in
order to grow within us. This is very clear in the New Testament.

The Lord Jesus came to sow Himself into the human heart. He is the sower and the seed. He sows Himself into our heart with the expectation that we would give Him the ground, the opportunity, to grow in us; then we grow by Him, with Him, and in Him. In addition, Matthew 13 shows us...that out of the growth comes transformation. In the parables in this chapter, there is first the sowing of the seed, then the growth of this life, and immediately there is transformation, which produces materials that are good for God's building. Therefore, three things are basically important: the birth of life, the growth of life, and the maturity of life, from which we have transformation. Then from this transformation we have the precious materials which are good for God's building.

The same thought is in 1 Corinthians 3. On the one hand, the apostle Paul says that we are co-workers with God doing the work of planting, so that God's cultivated land, God's harvest, may grow. Then on the other hand, we are builders to build God's house with the material produced from the growth of life (1 Cor. 3:6, 9, 12). This is also what is revealed in Matthew 13. However, we need the vision; otherwise, we can read this chapter time and again and still not see the birth of life, the growth of life, and transformation to produce the materials for the building of God.

The same thought is in 1 Peter 2. First we are the newborn babes who need to grow; then by this growth we are transformed into precious stones to be built up as a spiritual house (1 Pet. 2:2, 5). God's intention is to have a spiritual house, a building as His corporate expression. How can God accomplish this building? It is by sowing His Son Christ into us that He may grow in us and we may grow in Him and with Him in order to be transformed, changed in nature and in form, to be the precious materials for God's building. As Christians we need to be very clear about this. (*Practical Lessons on the Experience of Life*, pp. 197-199)

Further Reading: Life-study of 1 Peter, msg. 16; *Practical Lessons on the Experience of Life,* ch. 16; *The Stream,* vol. 12, no. 1, pp. 1-29; *The Crucial Revelation of Life in the Scriptures,* ch. 16

Enlightenment and inspiration: _____

_____

_____

Morning Nourishment

1 Pet. You yourselves also, as living stones, are being built
2:5   up as a spiritual house...
John   He led him to Jesus. Looking at him, Jesus said, You
1:42   are Simon, the son of John; you shall be called Cephas
       (which is interpreted, Peter).
Matt. ...Peter answered and said, You are the Christ, the
16:16-18 Son of the living God. And Jesus answered and said
       to him, Blessed are you, Simon Barjona, because flesh
       and blood has not revealed *this* to you, but My Father
       who is in the heavens. And I also say to you that you
       are Peter, and upon this rock I will build My church,
       and the gates of Hades shall not prevail against it.

[According to 1 Peter 2:5], we, the believers in Christ, are living stones, like Christ, through regeneration and transformation. We were created of clay (Rom. 9:21). But at regeneration we received the seed of the divine life, which by its growth in us transforms us into living stones. At Peter's conversion the Lord gave him a new name, Peter—a stone (John 1:42). When Peter received the revelation concerning Christ, the Lord revealed further that He also was the rock—a stone (Matt. 16:16-18). Peter was impressed by these two incidents that both Christ and His believers are stones for God's building.

By our natural birth we are clay, not stones....Genesis 2:7 says that man was made from the dust of the ground. Romans 9 reveals that we are vessels of clay. How, then, can we become stones? We become stones through the process of transformation. (*Life-study of 1 Peter,* p. 151)

Today's Reading

When Peter first met the Lord Jesus, the Lord changed his name from Simon to Peter [John 1:42]....According to biblical principle, whatever the Lord speaks will be. Therefore, when the Lord called Peter a stone, that meant that he would certainly become a stone. Whatever the Lord says to us will be fulfilled. If He says, "You are gold," then you will be golden. The Lord knew that when He changed Simon's name to Peter, a stone, he would become a stone.

In John 1:42 Peter was told that he was a stone. Then sometime later, in Caesarea Philippi, in answer to the Lord's question, "Who do you say that I am," Peter, receiving the revelation from the Father, said, "You are the Christ, the Son of the living God." To this the Lord Jesus replied, "And I also say to you that you are Peter, and upon this rock I will build My church..." (Matt. 16:18). Here the Lord indicates that He is the rock upon which the church is built and that Peter is a stone.

No doubt, these two incidents, the one recorded in John 1 and the other in Matthew 16, were deeply impressed into Peter's being. He could never forget those events. It must have been from these experiences that Peter obtained the concept of living stones for the building of the spiritual house, which is the church. When Peter wrote this portion of 1 Peter, he wrote it according to the impression these events made upon him.

First Peter 2:5 says that we, as living stones, are being built up a spiritual house. However, we all are clay. How can we be built up? In order to be built up a spiritual house, we need to become stones. But how can we actually become living stones? We become living stones by coming to Christ as the living stone (v. 4).

We may use petrified wood as an illustration of transformation. In Arizona there is a place called the petrified forest, an area that contains much petrified wood. Petrified wood is wood that has been changed into stone. Over a long period of time, water has been flowing over wood and through it. By means of this flow of water, the substance of the wood is changed into stone. On the one hand, the element of wood is carried away; on the other hand, the element of stone is brought in to replace the element of wood. In this way the wood becomes stone. (*Life-study of 1 Peter*, pp. 151-152)

Further Reading: Life-study of 1 Peter, msg. 18

Enlightenment and inspiration: _____

_____

_____

_____

Morning Nourishment

Eph. In whom all the building, being fitted together, is
2:21 growing into a holy temple in the Lord.

Psa. Search me, O God, and know my heart; try me, and
139:23-24 know my anxious thoughts; and see if there is some
harmful way in me, and lead me on the eternal way.

God's life...faces obstacles and difficulties in us. Every part of our entire being, both inwardly and outwardly, presents some obstacles to life. Although we know that God's life has come into us to be our life and to be lived out of us, in reality, this life encounters obstacles in us. Thus, it is very difficult for life to be lived out from us.

The first problem that God's life encounters in us is that we do not realize the darkness of our human concepts. We do not realize that our concepts, even though they seem proper and upright, are actually full of darkness and without life. Most Christians think that they should be zealous and forsake the world once they become Christians. From man's view, this sounds very logical. But without God, life, this is not practical.

Being a Christian is not a matter of zeal, nor a matter of spreading the gospel, nor a matter of forsaking the world, nor even a matter of not caring for material enjoyment. Being a Christian does not depend upon doing anything,...[but] upon how we take care of the Christ in us. The day we were saved, we received a living Christ, who became our life in us. From that day forward, our being a Christian has not depended on anything other than taking care of the living Christ in us. The only thing that matters is how we take care of the living Christ in us. (*Knowing Life and the Church*, pp. 27, 29-30)

Today's Reading

The second problem that life encounters in us is hypocrisy.... Whether or not a person's actions are of life...depends upon how he takes care of Christ....[A] brother may be born with a smooth personality like Jacob. A smooth stone does not have any sharp edges or protrusions. Some people are born this way; they never offend their siblings and parents at home, and they never offend their co-workers and superiors at work. Regardless of how people treat them, they are always smooth and even. When such a person is saved, he becomes a smooth Christian in the church. Three to five years may pass, and he never offends anyone. Many brothers and sisters praise him, saying, "This person is truly spiritual. He never argues at home or causes trouble outside. We see him doing many things, but he never gives his opinion. He is truly spiritual and full of life." This kind of speaking shows a lack of knowledge about life. We need to realize that this is actually hypocrisy. If his behavior were truly spiritual, then it would mean that he was spiritual even before he was saved. This is not possible. A person's spirituality is not determined by outward appearance but by how he takes care of Christ.

The third problem that life encounters in us is rebellion. Christ operates and moves in us in order to make us clear about His will and requirements for us and about His leading and dealing with us....Many times, we think that we are obeying the Lord, but actually we are rebelling against the Lord. For example, we may want to preach the gospel, but the Lord's operation in us is to pray. Since we do not like to stay at home and pray, but instead prefer to speak to gospel friends and fellowship with the brothers and sisters, we may simply act according to our desires. This is to act in rebellion.

We may be very active and zealous in doing those things but still may imprison the living Christ within us by ignoring Him....Our unwillingness to do things according to His will is clearly rebellion. ...Christ is living in us, and He is constantly giving us an inward sense of life. We should obey Him, but we often disobey Him. We often do not do what He wants us to do, and we often do what He does not want us to do....Rebellion continually creates obstacles for His life in us. (*Knowing Life and the Church,* pp. 32-33, 35-36)

Further Reading: Knowing Life and the Church, ch. 3; *Practical Lessons on the Experience of Life,* ch. 16*

Enlightenment and inspiration: _____

_____

_____

_____

Morning Nourishment

1 Cor. ...A soulish man does not receive the things of the
2:14-15 Spirit of God, for they are foolishness to him and he
is not able to know *them* because they are discerned
spiritually. But the spiritual man discerns all things,
but he himself is discerned by no one.

The fourth problem that life encounters in us is our natural
capability. Our natural being, disposition, and self are all problems that prevent God's life from coming out of us. However, the
problem of our natural capability and ability is even more serious.
...Many brothers and sisters truly love the Lord, are zealous for
the Lord, and are very godly. Nevertheless, their greatest problem
is the strength and greatness of their capabilities and abilities.
Consequently, Christ has no ground or way in them.

It is not easy for us to be aware of the problem of our natural
capability....When a person touches [some believers], he only senses
their capability and ability because they have never been broken
in their capability and ability. When he contacts them, he can only
say that they seek and pursue the Lord but that their natural
capability has not been broken. This is because the Lord is unable
to get through in them when He encounters their capability.

[Some] are capable and talented, but they do not consider these
things as sin or filthiness. They even think that these are good and
useful things to the church,...that they need such capabilities and
talent in order to serve God. They do not despise their natural capabilities; instead, they treasure them. If these capabilities remain
unbroken in them, they will become a problem to Christ's life.

There is one solution to all these obstacles in us—we must
pass through the cross and let the cross break us. If we want
Christ's life to be unhindered in us, we must experience the
breaking of the cross and allow these obstacles to be dealt with
and removed. This will allow Christ's life to be lived out from us.
(*Knowing Life and the Church*, pp. 36-37)

Today's Reading

In 1 Peter 2:1 Peter goes on to say, "Therefore putting away all malice and all guile and hypocrisies and envyings and all evil speakings." This verse begins with "therefore." This indicates that the exhortation in 2:1-10 is based upon what is unveiled in chapter one. Three main things accomplished in the believers by the Triune God are emphasized in chapter one: the Father's regeneration (vv. 3, 23), the Son's redemption (vv. 2, 18-19), and the Spirit's sanctification (v. 2) to make the believers a holy people, living a holy life (vv. 15-16). Based upon this, Peter charges the believers to grow in life (2:2) for the building up of a spiritual house (2:5).

Although chapter one is complete in itself, Peter, according to his experiences, still has more to say. Therefore, with chapter one as his basis, he proceeds to give the charge found in chapter two. He begins by telling the saints to put away all malice, guile, hypocrisies, envyings, and evil speakings. Of the hundreds of sinful things, Peter selects five: malice, guile, hypocrisy, envy, and evil speaking.

According to the sequence of these five matters, malice is the root, the source, and evil speaking is the expression. We may have malice as a root within us. Then there will eventually be evil speaking as the expression of this malice. The development from malice to evil speaking includes guile, hypocrisies, and envyings, three downward steps from malice toward evil speaking. If we have guile, we shall also have hypocrisies; and if hypocrisies, then envyings as well. Hence, the root is malice, the development includes guile, hypocrisy, and envy, and the final expression is evil speaking.

Not even a verse such as 2:1 should be read in a careless way. We should not take any verse for granted or neglect to study it seriously. Rather, we should study every verse with the goal and expectation of getting into the depths of it. Actually, the depths of the Word are the reality of the Word. This reality is the truth. If we consider verse 1 carefully, we shall see the root, the development, and the expression. In the light of this verse we see that all malice needs to be uprooted. (*Life-study of 1 Peter*, pp. 124-125)

Further Reading: Knowing Life and the Church, ch. 3

Enlightenment and inspiration: _____

_____

_____

_____

Morning Nourishment

1 Pet. **Therefore putting away all malice and all guile and**
2:1-3 **hypocrisies and envyings and all evil speakings, as**
newborn babes, long for the guileless milk of the
word in order that by it you may grow unto salva-
tion, if you have tasted that the Lord is good.

Born through regeneration (1 Pet. 1:3, 23), the believers become babes who can grow in life unto further salvation, and that for God's building, by being nourished with the spiritual milk.

Guileless milk is milk without false purpose, without any other goal but to nourish the soul....The milk of the word is not milk for the body, but is milk for the soul, the inner being. It is conveyed in the word of God to nourish our inner man through the understanding of our rational mind, and it is assimilated by our mental faculties.

The nourishment contained in the guileless milk of the word is an antibiotic for guile. In the Word of God there is a nourishment that is milk for our inner being. Just as our physical body is nourished with milk, so our inner being, our soul, needs to be nourished with the guileless milk of the word. This milk contains an element that can eliminate our guile. Therefore, the milk of the word is guileless milk.

The guileless milk of the word nourishes us, and by this nourishment we grow....We need to desire the guileless milk of the word so that by it we may have real growth in life. True growth is the increase of the measure of life. If we are growing in life, the life element within us will increase, and there will be an increase in our spiritual stature (Eph. 4:13). (*Life-study of 1 Peter,* pp. 125-126, 128-129)

Today's Reading

According to Peter's word in 1 Peter 2:2, by the guileless milk of the word we may grow unto salvation....To grow in life results in salvation. Salvation here, as the result of growth in life, is not initial salvation. God's full and complete salvation has a long span— from regeneration, including justification, to glorification (Rom. 8:30). At regeneration we received initial salvation. Then we need to grow by feeding on Christ as the nourishing milk in the word of

God unto full salvation, unto maturity for glorification. This will be the salvation of our soul, which will be revealed to us at the unveiling of the Lord Jesus (1:5, 9-10, 13). However, according to the context, "unto salvation" here refers directly to "being built up as a spiritual house into a holy priesthood to offer up spiritual sacrifices" in 2:5, and to telling out "the virtues of Him" in verse 9.

The salvation in verse 2...implies transformation. Regeneration is in the stage of initial salvation; transformation, in the stage of progressing salvation; and glorification, in the stage of consummation. We are not in the initial stage or in the stage of completion. We are in the progressing stage of salvation; that is, we are in the stage of transformation.

Transformation involves a change from one form into another form. However, it involves an inward change in nature or constitution, not simply an outward change in form. For example,...[an ill person] may try to improve his appearance by putting some kind of coloring on his face. I do not like that kind of skin coloring, for it makes me think of the work of a mortician, who tries to make the face of a dead person appear as attractive as possible. Today both disciples of Confucius and many Christians are involved in outward works of self-improvement, works that can be compared to those of a mortician. Such an outward change is altogether different from living, inward transformation.

Both regeneration in 1:23 and the newborn babes in 2:2 point to the same matter—regeneration with the divine life. This regeneration is the base for our growth in life and for the purification of our inner being. We all have within us the divine life that we received in regeneration as the basis of all spiritual growth. In order to grow and be purified, we must have this base. Therefore, as newborn babes, we should long for the guileless milk of the word so that by it we may grow unto transformation. (*Life-study of 1 Peter,* pp. 131-134)

Further Reading: Life-study of 1 Peter, msgs. 15-16; *Life-study of Exodus,* msg. 57

Enlightenment and inspiration: _____

_____

_____

_____

Morning Nourishment

1 Pet. You yourselves also, as living stones, are being built
2:5 up as a spiritual house into a holy priesthood to offer
up spiritual sacrifices acceptable to God through
Jesus Christ.
9 But you are a chosen race, a royal priesthood, a
holy nation, a people acquired for a possession, so
that you may tell out the virtues of Him who has
called you out of darkness into His marvelous light.

[In 1 Peter 2:9] *race, priesthood, nation,* and *people* are all collective nouns, referring to the believers corporately. As a race, the
believers have been chosen; as a priesthood, a body of priests, we are
royal, kingly; as a nation, we are holy; as a people, we are God's possession, a possession particularly acquired and owned by God as His
treasure. The chosen race denotes our lineage from God; the royal
priesthood, our service to God; the holy nation, our community for
God; and the people for a possession, our preciousness to God. This
is all in the corporate sense. Hence, we need to be built together.

The words *chosen race* indicate our source. As a chosen race,
we have our source in God. We are also a royal priesthood. *Royal*
denotes the status of our priesthood, which is kingly, like that of
Christ the King, our High Priest, typified by Melchisedec (Heb.
7:1-2, 25; Gen. 14:18). We are also a holy nation and a people for a
possession. *Holy* denotes the nature of the nation.... *A people for a
possession*...implies a particular treasure. We are God's particular treasure, His special and precious possession....This is an
expression borrowed from the Old Testament (Deut. 7:6; 14:2;
26:18), and it denotes a people privately possessed by God as His
peculiar treasure (Exo. 19:5), His own possession. First we are a
chosen race, then a royal priesthood, a holy nation, and a people
for a possession. As God's particular treasure, we are His people
who are precious to Him. (*Life-study of 1 Peter,* pp. 155-156)

Today's Reading

We are such a race, priesthood, nation, and people so that we
may tell out the virtues of Him who has called us out of darkness

into His marvelous light. The Greek word rendered *tell out* also means "proclaim abroad." First we must be born anew and grow in life, and then be built up and serve corporately. Now we need to proclaim abroad, to tell out. To serve corporately is to satisfy God by offering up Christ as spiritual sacrifices; to proclaim abroad is to benefit others by showing forth the virtues of the One who has called us out of darkness into His marvelous light [1 Pet. 2:9].

The virtues here are excellent attributes, acts, and behavior. God has many virtues....All the excellent divine attributes are the virtues of God. We need to tell out, to proclaim abroad, these excellent virtues.

The apostles proclaimed the virtues of the Lord. They preached them, they taught them, and they announced them. Whatever the apostles preached and taught was a telling out of the virtues they had seen and enjoyed. It was a proclaiming abroad of the virtues in which they had participated. This is what it means to tell out God's excellencies. Today we need to follow the apostles to tell out the excellent virtues of the Lord.

According to 2:5, the building up of a spiritual house into a holy priesthood is for a particular function. This function is "to offer up spiritual sacrifices acceptable to God through Jesus Christ." Here we see that Jesus Christ is the channel through which the spiritual sacrifices are offered to God. (*Life-study of 1 Peter,* pp. 156-157, 155)

The spiritual sacrifices that the believers offer in the New Testament age according to God's economy are: (1) Christ as the reality of all the sacrifices of the Old Testament types, such as the burnt offering, meal offering, peace offering, sin offering, and trespass offering (Lev. 1—5); (2) the sinners saved by our gospel preaching, offered as members of Christ (Rom. 15:16); and (3) our body, our praises, and the things that we do for God (Rom. 12:1; Heb. 13:15-16; Phil. 4:18). (1 Pet. 2:5, footnote 8)

Further Reading: Life-study of 1 Peter, msg. 18; *Life-study of 2 Corinthians,* msg. 51; *Knowing Life and the Church,* ch. 16

Enlightenment and inspiration: _____
_____
_____
_____

Hymns, #913

1   Serve and work within the Body,
    This the Lord doth signify;
  For His purpose is the Body,
    And with it we must comply.

    Serve and work within the Body,
      Never independently;
    As the members of the Body,
      Functioning relatedly.

2   As the members we've been quickened
    Not as individuals free;
  We must always serve together,
    All related mutually.

3   Living stones, we're built together
    And a house for God must be,
  As the holy priesthood serving,
    In a blessed harmony.

4   Thus we must be built together,
    In position minister;
  For the basis of our service
    Is the body character.

5   In our ministry and service,
    From the Body, our supply;
  If detached and isolated,
    Out of function, we will die.

6   'Tis by serving in the Body
    Riches of the Head we share;
  'Tis by functioning as members
    Christ's full measure we will bear.

7   To the Head fast holding ever,
    That we may together grow,
  From the Head supplies incoming
    Thru us to the Body flow.

8   Lord, anew we give our bodies;
    May we be transformed to prove
  All Thy will, to know Thy Body,
    And therein to serve and move.

Composition for prophecy with main point and sub-points: _____

_____
_____
_____
_____
_____
_____
_____
_____
_____
_____
_____
_____
_____
_____
_____
_____
_____
_____
_____
_____
_____
_____
_____
_____
_____
_____
_____
_____
_____
_____
_____
_____
_____

Becoming a Reproduction of Christ and Being Holy in All Our Manner of Life

Scripture Reading: 1 Pet. 1:15; 2:12, 21; Rom. 8:29; Gal. 2:20; 4:19; Eph. 3:16-17a

Day 1

I. As believers in Christ, we may become a reproduction of Christ as our model (1 Pet. 2:21):

A. The living of the Lord Jesus under the government of God is a model so that we may follow in His steps by becoming His reproduction (vv. 21-23; Eph. 4:20-21).

B. The Greek word for *model* in 1 Peter 2:21 denotes a master copy used in the teaching of writing—a writing copy, an underwriting, for students to use in tracing letters as they learn to draw them:

1. The Lord Jesus has set His life before us as an underwriting for us to copy by tracing and following His steps (Matt. 11:28-30).

2. It is not God's intention that we try to imitate Christ by our own effort; what we need is not imitation but reproduction (Rom. 8:29; 2 Cor. 3:18).

C. We need to become Christ's reproduction, copies of Christ, by a process that involves the riches of the divine life; when this process is completed, we will become a reproduction of Christ (John 3:15; Eph. 3:8).

Day 2

D. The making of Xerox copies may be used to illustrate what Peter means by Christ being a model for us:

1. As a model, Christ is the original used in spiritual Xeroxing to make us a reproduction of Himself (Rom. 8:29).

2. In this process the Spirit of Christ is the light, and the riches of the divine life are the inking substance.

3. As the "paper" we are put under the light of the Holy Spirit, and we pass through the

inking substance to become a reproduction,
a living copy of the original, a reproduction
of Christ.

Day 3   E. In order to become a reproduction of Christ as
our model, we need to experience Christ as the
One living in us, being formed in us, and making
His home in our hearts (Gal. 2:20; 4:19; Eph.
3:16-17a):

1. The New Testament reveals that Christ is
   deeply related to our inner being (Gal. 1:16;
   Col. 3:10-11).

2. The pneumatic Christ—Christ as the life-
   giving Spirit—is living in us (1 Cor. 15:45b;
   Gal. 2:20):

   a. God's economy is that the "I" be crucified
      in Christ's death and that Christ live in
      us in His resurrection (John 14:19).

   b. We are one spirit with the Lord, we have
      one life with Him, and we should now
      be one person with Him (1 Cor. 6:17; Col.
      3:4; Phil. 1:21a).

   c. Since Christ dwells in us as the Spirit, we
      need to let Him live in us (John 14:16-19;
      Gal. 2:20).

Day 4   3. To have Christ formed in us is to have
   Christ fully grown in us (4:19):

   a. Christ was born into us at the time we
      repented and believed in Him, then He
      lives in us in our Christian life, and finally,
      He will be formed in us at our maturity
      (John 1:12-13; 3:15; Gal. 2:20).

   b. To have Christ formed in us is to allow
      the all-inclusive Spirit to occupy every
      part of our inner being, to have Christ
      fully grown in us (Col. 2:19; Eph. 4:15-16).

   c. To have Christ formed in us implies that
      we are being constituted with Christ or-
      ganically (Col. 3:10-11).

   d. *Formed* in Galatians 4:19 corresponds to

image in 2 Corinthians 3:18; Christ will be formed in us so that we may express Him in His image.

4. The Christ who lives in us and who is being formed in us is making His home in our hearts (Eph. 3:16-17a):

   a. Christ wants to make His home deep down in our being; He desires to spread from our spirit to all the parts of our heart.

   b. The more Christ spreads within us, the more He settles down in us and makes His home in our hearts; in this way He occupies every part of our inner being, possessing these parts and saturating them with Himself so that we may be filled unto all the fullness of God (v. 19b).

Day 5

5. As Christ lives in us, is formed in us, and makes His home in our hearts, we become a reproduction of Christ for the corporate expression of God (Rom. 8:29; 12:4-5; Rev. 21:2).

II. **As we become a reproduction of Christ, we will have a manner of life that expresses the Triune God, and we will be holy in all our manner of life (1 Pet. 1:15; 2:12):**

A. The expression of the Triune God from within a believer indicates that such a believer has become a reproduction of Christ (Phil. 1:20).

B. The excellent manner of life—a life beautiful in its virtues—is the holy manner of life and the good manner of life in Christ, a life not only for God but filled and saturated with God (1 Pet. 2:12; 1:15; 3:16).

C. A holy manner of life is a life that expresses the holy nature of God (1:15).

D. According to 1:15, we should not merely be holy and live a holy life—we should become holy in all our manner of life.

E. If we would be holy in all our manner of life, we ourselves, the persons, must become holy; our being, our disposition, our entire person, should become holy.

Day 6

F. If we would be holy in all our manner of life, we need to be habitually holy; we need to become a certain kind of person, a person who is holy in constitution.

G. In order to be holy in all our manner of life, we need the impartation of the Father's holy nature into us, the sanctifying work of the Holy Spirit to make us holy, and God's discipline so that we may partake of His holiness (vv. 2-3, 15; Heb. 12:10):

1. When we were regenerated, the Father imparted His holy nature into us as the basic factor for us to be holy in all our manner of life (1 Pet. 1:3, 15).

2. We become holy in all our manner of life through the sanctification of the Spirit; with the Father's holy nature within us as the basis of operation, the Holy Spirit is working on us to make us holy (v. 2).

3. Because we are often disobedient, we need God's discipline; for this reason, Hebrews 12:10 says that God the Father disciplines us so that we may partake of His holiness and become holy even as He is holy (1 Pet. 1:15-16).

Morning Nourishment

1 Pet.   ...But if, while doing good and suffering, you endure,
2:20-23   this is grace with God. For to this you were called,
because Christ also suffered on your behalf, leaving
you a model so that you may follow in His steps; who
committed no sin, nor was guile found in His mouth;
who being reviled did not revile in return; suffering,
He did not threaten but kept committing *all* to Him
who judges righteously.

Peter's thought in 1 Peter 2:21 is deep. In order to appreciate the
worth of a verse such as this, we need experience. If we do not have
adequate Christian experience, we shall not understand what
Peter says concerning grace and concerning Christ as our model.

He is the master copy, the original copy, and...through a process
of spiritual Xeroxing we are becoming a reproduction of Christ.
...While the Lord Jesus was on earth suffering, He kept committing all to the One who judges righteously. This brief word indicates not only that the Lord lived a life that was a model for us,
but also that He lived a life absolutely under God's government.
He Himself was always under the government of God, and He
committed everything related to Him to God's judgment. (*Life-
study of 1 Peter,* pp. 183, 185-186)

Today's Reading

The word *model* [in 1 Peter 2:21] has been spoiled by common
usage. Literally, the Greek word means a writing-copy, an underwriting for students to use in tracing letters as they learn to draw
them. In ancient times teachers would write letters on writing
material, and those letters became a master copy. Another piece of
writing material was put upon the master copy. Then the children
would practice writing by tracing the letters from the master copy
onto their copy....The Lord Jesus has set His life before us as an
underwriting for us to copy by tracing and following His steps.

It is not God's intention, however, that we try to imitate Christ
by our own effort. We know from experience that trying to imitate
Christ does not work. We are not able to imitate Him. What we

need is not imitation, but reproduction. There is a great difference between imitation and reproduction. Outwardly Christ is our model, and inwardly He is our person, living in us, being formed in us, and making His home in us. Through this process we become a reproduction of the original, a reproduction of Christ as our model.

We need to become Christ's reproduction, copies of Christ, by experiencing a process that involves the riches of the divine life. When this process is completed, we shall become a reproduction of Christ. When anyone observes the expression of the Triune God from within a believer, this indicates that such a believer has become a reproduction of Christ, the model. The manner of life that expresses the processed Triune God is a reproduction of Christ.

As a model to the believers, Christ is the original used for making a reproduction of Himself. In order to understand Christ as our model, we need experience. From experience we know that as we enjoy Christ day by day, we are undergoing the process of spiritual reproduction to make us living copies of Christ.

To become the reproduction of Christ is very different from trying to imitate Him. To illustrate, a man may set an example for a monkey to stand upright, and the monkey stands up, imitating the man. Then the man walks, and the monkey imitates him by walking on two feet. But after the imitation is finished, the man leaves, and the monkey goes back to walking on all fours. At least to a certain extent, those teachers who instruct believers to imitate Christ are like a man training a monkey to imitate a human being. Trying to imitate Christ in such a way simply does not work. Therefore, I do not encourage you to imitate Christ. Instead, I would point you to His riches. I would point you to Him as the One living in us, being formed in us, and making His home in us so that we may undergo the process of becoming the reproduction of Christ as our model. (*The Conclusion of the New Testament,* pp. 600-602)

Further Reading: The Conclusion of the New Testament, msg. 56; *Life-study of 1 Peter,* msg. 21

Enlightenment and inspiration: _____

_____

_____

_____

Morning Nourishment

Matt.   Come to Me all who toil and are burdened, and I will
11:28-29 give you rest. Take My yoke upon you and learn from
Me, for I am meek and lowly in heart, and you will
find rest for your souls.

Rom.   Because those whom He foreknew, He also predesti-
8:29 nated *to be* conformed to the image of His Son, that
He might be the Firstborn among many brothers.

The processed and consummated Triune God passed through human living to set up a model for the many upcoming God-men—being crucified to live that God might be expressed through humanity. This is clearly unveiled in 1 Peter 2:21, which tells us that Christ in His human living left us a model, an example, for us to copy. Christ Jesus, while He was on this earth, set up a copy for spiritual Xeroxing. He was the model, the copy, for Xeroxing, to produce millions of copies. (*The Practical Way to Live a Life according to the High Peak of the Divine Revelation in the Holy Scriptures,* p. 15)

Today's Reading

First Peter 2:21 clearly says that we have been called to suffer unjustly because Christ suffered on our behalf and left us a model so that we should follow in His steps.

The making of Xerox copies may be used to illustrate what Peter means by Christ being a model for us....Christ's living revealed in the four Gospels is the master copy used in this spiritual Xeroxing. For Xeroxing, we must first have an original. The Xeroxed copy made from this original is a reproduction, not an imitation. We know from experience that trying to imitate Christ does not work. We are not able to imitate Him. What we need is not imitation but reproduction.

I have heard an explanation of how the Xeroxing process operates. First there is the need of a proper light to expose the original copy. Then there is the need of a special kind of ink, called toner. Besides this, there is the need of a heat roller and the paper upon which to make the copy. This paper, of course, must be clean. Then this clean paper is exposed under the light to the copy. Through the light, the heat, and the proper ink, whatever the copy is will be reproduced onto the paper. The result is reproduction, not imitation.

In the process of spiritual Xeroxing, the Spirit of Christ is the light, and the riches of the divine life are the inking substance. We are the paper on which the reproduction of the original is to be made. This paper must be put under the light of the Holy Spirit, and it must pass through the inking substance in order to have the original copy—Christ Himself—reproduced on it. Through this process we eventually become a reproduction of the original, a reproduction of Christ.

We have pointed out that the paper used in Xeroxing must be clean. It should not have anything on it....Peter refers to this clean "paper" in 1:22, where he speaks about the purifying of our souls. Much of what Peter writes in chapters one and two is related to producing clean paper for spiritual Xeroxing.

Christ is not merely a model for us to follow outwardly. He is a writing-copy, an original for spiritual Xeroxing, and we need to become His reproduction. This means that we should become Xerox copies of Christ by experiencing a process that involves spiritual light and the riches of the divine life. The result of this process is that we eventually become a reproduction of Christ.

At least to a certain extent, those Christian teachers who instruct believers to imitate Christ are like a man training a monkey to imitate a human being. I have learned that trying to imitate Christ simply does not work. In these messages I am not encouraging you to imitate the Lord. On the contrary, I am pointing you to the riches of Christ and the beauty of the Lord. Furthermore, both the heavenly light and the spiritual ink are available to us, and we are all undergoing the process of spiritual Xeroxing. (*Life-study of 1 Peter,* pp. 180-183)

Further Reading: Life-study of 1 Peter, msg. 20; *Life-study of Romans,* msg. 52

Enlightenment and inspiration: _____

_____

_____

_____

Morning Nourishment

Gal. I am crucified with Christ; and *it is* no longer I *who*
2:20 live, but *it is* Christ *who* lives in me; and the *life* which
        I now live in the flesh I live in faith, the *faith* of the Son
        of God, who loved me and gave Himself up for me.
John Yet a little while and the world beholds Me no longer,
14:19 but you behold Me; because I live, you also shall live.
Phil. For to me, to live is Christ...
1:21

Only when Christ is formed within us by expanding and
increasing into every part of our being, can He make His home in
our hearts; and only when Christ has made His home in our
hearts, will we have the measure of the stature of the fullness of
Christ. First Christ is revealed in us. Then He lives within us, is
formed within us, and makes His home in our hearts. Finally the
result of Christ being revealed in us, living in us, being formed in
us, and making His home in our hearts is that we arrive at the
measure of the stature of the fullness of Christ. This is what God
planned and intended in eternity past for a Christian to be—a
person who is full of Christ. (*The Mystery of God and the Mystery
of Christ*, p. 65)

Today's Reading

Christ is not only our life; He as a person lives in us. All Christians need to realize that we have another person—Christ—
living in us. We need to see the vision that the very One who died
on the cross to redeem us is now living within us.

Christ, on the one hand, is in the third heavens. But on the
other hand, He lives within us. Christ became the life-giving
Spirit in order that He might live in us. Without being the life-
giving Spirit, it would not be possible for the heavenly Christ to
live in us. According to the New Testament revelation, Christ is
both the ascended Lord and the life-giving Spirit. As the ascended
Lord He is sitting in the heavens at the right hand of God, and as
the life-giving Spirit He lives within us....Because He lives in us,
we should take Him as our person and live Him.

In Galatians 2:20 Paul says, "Christ...lives in me." We need a proper understanding of what it means for Christ to live in us. It is rather easy to understand that Christ lives, but it is difficult to understand how Christ lives in us. For Christ to live in us does not mean that He lives instead of us. In Galatians 2:20 Paul says, on the one hand, "no longer I," and on the other hand, "Christ…lives in me." The phrase "in me" is of great importance. Yes, it is Christ who lives, but He lives in us.

In order to understand how Christ can live in us, we need to consider John 14. Before His death and resurrection, the Lord Jesus said to the disciples, "Because I live, you also shall live" (v. 19). Christ lives in us by causing us to live with Him. Christ does not live alone; He lives in us and with us. He lives in us by enabling us to live with Him. In a very real sense, if we do not live with Him, He cannot live in us. We have not been altogether ruled out, and our life has not been exchanged for the divine life. We continue to exist, but we exist with the Triune God. The Triune God who now dwells within us causes us to live with Christ. Hence, Christ lives in us through our living with Him.

Paul's word in Galatians 2:20 about Christ living in us is definite and emphatic. There is no ambiguity here. Paul clearly says that Christ, as a person, lives in us. This Christ who lives in us is the pneumatic Christ, the Christ who is the Spirit. Now that He dwells in us as the Spirit, we need to learn how to let Him live in us and how to live together with Him. A normal believer is a person who has one life and one living with Christ. We are one spirit with Him (1 Cor. 6:17), we have one life with Him, and now we should be one person with Him. Sooner or later, those who seek the Lord realize that Someone divine, heavenly, eternal, and spiritual lives in them as a person. If we see this, we shall also see that just as He lived because of the Father, we should now live because of Him, taking Him as our person. (*The Conclusion of the New Testament,* pp. 587-589)

Further Reading: The Conclusion of the New Testament, msg. 55; *The Mystery of God and the Mystery of Christ,* ch. 6

Enlightenment and inspiration: _____

_____

_____

Morning Nourishment

Gal. **My children, with whom I travail again in birth**
4:19 **until Christ is formed in you.**
Eph. **That He would grant you, according to the riches**
3:16-17 **of His glory, to be strengthened with power through**
His Spirit into the inner man, that Christ may
make His home in your hearts through faith...

Christ lives in the believers for them to have Him formed in them. In Galatians 4:19,...to have Christ formed in us requires transformation. According to...Galatians, Christ has been revealed in us (1:16), He is now living in us (2:20), and He will be formed in us. To have Christ formed in us is to have Christ grown in us in full. First, Christ was born into us at our regeneration, now He lives in us in our Christian life, and He will be formed in us at our maturity. (*The Conclusion of the New Testament*, p. 1539)

Today's Reading

Paul's word about Christ being formed in the believers implies that we are being constituted of Christ. Christ is living in us, He is being formed in us, and He is becoming our constitution. To have Christ formed in us is a living, organic matter. Christ is now living in us so that we may be constituted of Him organically. He intends to constitute our whole being—our mind, emotion, and will—of Himself. Eventually, our whole being will be constituted of the element of Christ....He will constitute every part of our soul so that we may have His form, His image, in every part of our being.

For Christ to be formed in us means that His element is being constituted into us. In other words, His constitution is becoming our constitution. This is not merely a matter of the element of Christ being within us but of having the element of Christ constituted into us. To be constituted of Christ in this way involves a process of organic transformation and formation.

The word *formed* in Galatians 4:19 corresponds to the word *image* in 2 Corinthians 3:18, where Paul tells us that we are being transformed into Christ's image. This image is a form. Christ must be formed in us so that we may express Him by being in His image. As the living One, He with His element is working within us organically, constituting Himself into our being so that we may have His form and express His image.

Ephesians 3:17a indicates that Christ lives in the believers for them to have Him making His home in their hearts....Through regeneration Christ came into our spirit (2 Tim. 4:22), and now we should allow Him to spread Himself into every part of our hearts. The heart is the totality of our inward parts and the center of our inward being. Therefore, when Christ makes His home in our hearts, He controls our entire inward being and supplies and strengthens every inward part with Himself.

The Greek word rendered *make home* in Ephesians 3:17 is the word for house plus a prefix that means "down." This indicates that Christ wants to make His home deep down in our being. As we are strengthened into the inner man, the way is opened for Christ to spread in us, to spread from our spirit to every part of our mind, emotion, and will. The more Christ spreads within us, the more He settles down in us and makes His home in us. This means that He occupies every part of our inner being, possessing all these parts and saturating them with Himself.

In order for this to take place, Christ must occupy every part of our being. We may compare our heart to a house with many rooms. One room is the mind, and other rooms are the emotion, the will, and the conscience. We have believed in the Lord Jesus, and we have Him within us, but He still needs to make His home in our heart. Although we have Christ in us in a general way, we may not have Him in us in a particular way, saturating our mind, emotion, will, and conscience. Christ desires to make His home in our heart, to occupy every part of our inner being. Our inner being, therefore, needs to be saturated, possessed, occupied, and filled with Christ. (*The Conclusion of the New Testament*, pp. 1539-1540, 1556-1557)

Further Reading: The Conclusion of the New Testament, msgs. 142-143; *Life-study of Galatians*, msg. 23

Enlightenment and inspiration: _____

_____

_____

_____

Morning Nourishment

1 Pet. But according to the Holy One who called you, you
1:15 yourselves also be holy in all *your* manner of life.
2:12 Having your manner of life excellent among the
Gentiles, so that in the matter concerning which
they speak against you as evildoers they may, by
your good works, as they see *them* with their own
eyes, glorify God in the day of *His* visitation.
3:16 ...Having a good conscience, so that in the matter in
which you are spoken against, those who revile your
good manner of life in Christ may be put to shame.

With His firstborn Son as the base, pattern, element, and
means, God is producing many sons, and the many sons who are
produced are the many believers who believe into God's firstborn
Son and are joined to Him as one. They are exactly like Him in life
and nature, and, like Him, they have both humanity and divinity.
They are His increase and expression in order that they may
express the eternal Triune God for eternity. The church today is a
miniature of this expression (Eph. 1:23), and the New Jerusalem
in eternity will be the ultimate manifestation of this expression
(Rev. 21:11). (Rom. 8:29, footnote 4)

Today's Reading

[In 1 Peter 1:14 Peter says], "As children of obedience, do not be
fashioned according to the former lusts in your ignorance."...*Do
not be fashioned* denotes a state that is a path on which God's
elect, as sojourners, walk. We should not be fashioned according
to the former lusts. This means that we should not shape ourselves according to them. Formerly, we were ignorant. But now,
having become children of obedience, we are knowledgeable.

[In verse 15] *the Holy One* is the Triune God—the choosing
Father, the redeeming Son, and the sanctifying Spirit (vv. 1-2). The
Father has regenerated His elect, imparting His holy nature into
them (v. 3); the Son has redeemed them with His blood from the vain
manner of life (vv. 18-19); and the Spirit has sanctified them according to the Father's holy nature, separating them from anything

other than God, that they, by the holy nature of the Father, may become holy in all their manner of life, even as holy as God Himself.

We become holy in all our manner of life through the sanctification of the Spirit. This is based on regeneration, which brings us the holy nature of God and issues in a holy life.

We ourselves need to become holy. This is not merely a matter of wearing a certain kind of clothing or of not wearing makeup. That concept of holiness is too outward. Our being, our disposition, our entire person, should become holy. This is for us to become holy in all our manner of life.

In verse 16 Peter gives us the reason we need to become holy: "Because it is written, 'You shall be holy, because I am holy.'"

The Holy One who has called us as the Father has regenerated us to produce a holy family—a holy Father with holy children. As holy children, we should walk in a holy manner of life.

In 2:12 Peter goes on to say, "Having your manner of life excellent among the Gentiles, so that in the matter concerning which they speak against you as evildoers they may, by your good works, as they see them with their own eyes, glorify God in the day of His visitation." The manner of life here must be the holy manner of life (1:15) and the good manner of life in Christ (3:16), a life not only for God but filled and saturated with God. This manner of life is versus the vain manner of life of the unbelievers (1:18). The believers' manner of life should be excellent; that is, it should be beautiful in its virtues. We need to have such a life among the nations, among the Gentiles. Many versions render the Greek word for nations in verse 12 as Gentiles. Actually, the Greek word means nations. All the nations are Gentiles.

Christ is the life within us, and He is also the model for us to follow. If we live by Christ as our inward life, that is, by the indwelling Christ Himself, we shall undergo the process of spiritual Xeroxing to become a reproduction of Christ. (*Life-study of 1 Peter,* pp. 90-91, 167, 194)

Further Reading: Life-study of 1 Peter, msgs. 11, 19

Enlightenment and inspiration: *By His Life imparting me are regenerated, Sanctified unto Him . As " " the duplicating, reproducing and multiplying is accomplished*

Morning Nourishment

1 Pet. Chosen according to the foreknowledge of God the
1:2 Father in the sanctification of the Spirit unto the
obedience and sprinkling of the blood of Jesus
Christ: Grace to you and peace be multiplied.
16 Because it is written, "You shall be holy because I am
holy."
Heb. For they disciplined for a few days as it seemed good
12:10 to them; but He, for what is profitable that we might
partake of His holiness.

I would like to say a further word concerning the matter of becoming holy in all our manner of life (1 Pet. 1:15). The phrase *manner of life* is a literal translation of the Greek. According to 1:15, we should not merely be holy and live a holy life; we should become holy in all our manner of life. Others should be able to see a certain manner in our living, and this manner should be holy. This does not mean that we are holy occasionally or that we are holy in certain things. For instance, it is not that in the morning we are holy in one matter, and then later in the day we are no longer holy in that matter....If we would have a holy manner of life, we need to be habitually holy in our constitution. This means that we need to become a certain kind of person, a person who is holy in constitution. (*Life-study of 1 Peter,* p. 95)

Today's Reading

We may use fruit trees as an illustration of what we mean by a holy manner of life. An apple tree produces apples according to the apple-tree manner of life. Likewise, an orange tree produces oranges according to its manner of life. The producing of apples by an apple tree and oranges by an orange tree is not accidental. On the contrary, it is altogether according to the manner of life characteristic of each tree.

The same should be true of our becoming holy in our manner of life. Some Christians who emphasize a so-called holiness may sometimes act holy, but at other times they may be very worldly or fleshly. This indicates that they do not have a holy manner of life. To have a holy manner of life is to have a life that is the expression of God. It is to have a living that is the expression of the holy nature of God.

When we were regenerated, the holy nature of the Father was imparted to us. This holy nature that is now within us is the basic factor for us to live a holy manner of life. Once again we may use fruit trees as an illustration. If an apple tree did not have the life of an apple tree, it could not possibly have the manner of life of an apple tree. Suppose someone tried to attach apples to the branches of another kind of tree. After a short period of time, the apples would fall down. But an apple tree, having an apple-tree manner of life, expresses the nature of the apple tree that is within it. The principle is the same with becoming holy in all our manner of life. The Father has imparted His holy nature into us, and this is what makes it possible for us to have a life that expresses the holy God.

Second, concerning a holy manner of life, the Holy Spirit is doing a sanctifying work within us. The Greek word for sanctify is the verb form of the adjective holy. When the Holy Spirit sanctifies us, He makes us holy. With the Father's holy nature within us as a basis of operation, the Holy Spirit is working in us to make us holy.

Third, because we are often disobedient, we need God's discipline. For this reason, Hebrews 12:10 says that God the Father disciplines us so that we may partake of His holiness.

To have a holy manner of life, we need three things: the impartation of the Father's holy nature into our being, the sanctifying work of the Holy Spirit to make us holy, and God's discipline so that we may participate in the holiness of our holy God. These are the three factors for us to live a life of holiness. Our living should not only be holy to a certain extent, but our very manner of life should be holy. This means that we should have a living that is the expression of our holy God. (*Life-study of 1 Peter,* pp. 95-96)

Further Reading: Life-study of 1 Peter, msg. 12; *The Conclusion of the New Testament,* msg. 145

Enlightenment and inspiration: _____

_____

_____

_____

Hymns, #203

1   In the bosom of the Father,
      Ere the ages had begun,
    Thou wast in the Father's glory,
      God's unique begotten Son.
    When to us the Father gave Thee,
      Thou in person wast the same,
    All the fulness of the Father
      In the Spirit to proclaim.

2   By Thy death and resurrection,
      Thou wast made God's firstborn Son;
    By Thy life to us imparting,
      Was Thy duplication done.
    We, in Thee regenerated,
      Many sons to God became;
    Truly as Thy many brethren,
      We are as Thyself the same.

3   Once Thou wast the only grain, Lord,
      Falling to the earth to die,
    That thru death and resurrection
      Thou in life may multiply.
    We were brought forth in Thy nature
      And the many grains became;
    As one loaf we all are blended,
      All Thy fulness to proclaim.

4   We're Thy total reproduction,
      Thy dear Body and Thy Bride,
    Thine expression and Thy fulness,
      For Thee ever to abide.
    We are Thy continuation,
      Thy life-increase and Thy spread,
    Thy full growth and Thy rich surplus,
      One with Thee, our glorious Head.

*Composition for prophecy with main point and
sub-points:* _____

_____

_____

_____

_____

_____

_____

_____

_____

_____

_____

_____

_____

_____

_____

_____

_____

_____

_____

_____

_____

_____

_____

_____

_____

_____

_____

_____

_____

_____

_____

_____

_____

Reading Schedule for the Recovery Version of the Old Testament with Footnotes

Wk.	Lord's Day	Monday	Tuesday	Wednesday	Thursday	Friday	Saturday
1	Gen 1:1-5 ☐	1:6-23 ☐	1:24-31 ☐	2:1-9 ☐	2:10-25 ☐	3:1-13 ☐	3:14-24 ☐
2	4:1-26 ☐	5:1-32 ☐	6:1-22 ☐	7:1—8:3 ☐	8:4-22 ☐	9:1-29 ☐	10:1-32 ☐
3	11:1-32 ☐	12:1-20 ☐	13:1-18 ☐	14:1-24 ☐	15:1-21 ☐	16:1-16 ☐	17:1-27 ☐
4	18:1-33 ☐	19:1-38 ☐	20:1-18 ☐	21:1-34 ☐	22:1-24 ☐	23:1—24:27 ☐	24:28-67 ☐
5	25:1-34 ☐	26:1-35 ☐	27:1-46 ☐	28:1-22 ☐	29:1-35 ☐	30:1-43 ☐	31:1-55 ☐
6	32:1-32 ☐	33:1—34:31 ☐	35:1-29 ☐	36:1-43 ☐	37:1-36 ☐	38:1—39:23 ☐	40:1—41:13 ☐
7	41:14-57 ☐	42:1-38 ☐	43:1-34 ☐	44:1-34 ☐	45:1-28 ☐	46:1-34 ☐	47:1-31 ☐
8	48:1-22 ☐	49:1-15 ☐	49:16-33 ☐	50:1-26 ☐	Exo 1:1-22 ☐	2:1-25 ☐	3:1-22 ☐
9	4:1-31 ☐	5:1-23 ☐	6:1-30 ☐	7:1-25 ☐	8:1-32 ☐	9:1-35 ☐	10:1-29 ☐
10	11:1-10 ☐	12:1-14 ☐	12:15-36 ☐	12:37-51 ☐	13:1-22 ☐	14:1-31 ☐	15:1-27 ☐
11	16:1-36 ☐	17:1-16 ☐	18:1-27 ☐	19:1-25 ☐	20:1-26 ☐	21:1-36 ☐	22:1-31 ☐
12	23:1-33 ☐	24:1-18 ☐	25:1-22 ☐	25:23-40 ☐	26:1-14 ☐	26:15-37 ☐	27:1-21 ☐
13	28:1-21 ☐	28:22-43 ☐	29:1-21 ☐	29:22-46 ☐	30:1-10 ☐	30:11-38 ☐	31:1-17 ☐
14	31:18—32:35 ☐	33:1-23 ☐	34:1-35 ☐	35:1-35 ☐	36:1-38 ☐	37:1-29 ☐	38:1-31 ☐
15	39:1-43 ☐	40:1-38 ☐	Lev 1:1-17 ☐	2:1-16 ☐	3:1-17 ☐	4:1-35 ☐	5:1-19 ☐
16	6:1-30 ☐	7:1-38 ☐	8:1-36 ☐	9:1-24 ☐	10:1-20 ☐	11:1-47 ☐	12:1-8 ☐
17	13:1-28 ☐	13:29-59 ☐	14:1-18 ☐	14:19-32 ☐	14:33-57 ☐	15:1-33 ☐	16:1-17 ☐
18	16:18-34 ☐	17:1-16 ☐	18:1-30 ☐	19:1-37 ☐	20:1-27 ☐	21:1-24 ☐	22:1-33 ☐
19	23:1-22 ☐	23:23-44 ☐	24:1-23 ☐	25:1-23 ☐	25:24-55 ☐	26:1-24 ☐	26:25-46 ☐
20	27:1-34 ☐	Num 1:1-54 ☐	2:1-34 ☐	3:1-51 ☐	4:1-49 ☐	5:1-31 ☐	6:1-27 ☐
21	7:1-41 ☐	7:42-88 ☐	7:89—8:26 ☐	9:1-23 ☐	10:1-36 ☐	11:1-35 ☐	12:1—13:33 ☐
22	14:1-45 ☐	15:1-41 ☐	16:1-50 ☐	17:1—18:7 ☐	18:8-32 ☐	19:1-22 ☐	20:1-29 ☐
23	21:1-35 ☐	22:1-41 ☐	23:1-30 ☐	24:1-25 ☐	25:1-18 ☐	26:1-65 ☐	27:1-23 ☐
24	28:1-31 ☐	29:1-40 ☐	30:1—31:24 ☐	31:25-54 ☐	32:1-42 ☐	33:1-56 ☐	34:1-29 ☐
25	35:1-34 ☐	36:1-13 ☐	Deut 1:1-46 ☐	2:1-37 ☐	3:1-29 ☐	4:1-49 ☐	5:1-33 ☐
26	6:1—7:26 ☐	8:1-20 ☐	9:1-29 ☐	10:1-22 ☐	11:1-32 ☐	12:1-32 ☐	13:1—14:21 ☐

Reading Schedule for the Recovery Version of the Old Testament with Footnotes

Wk.	Lord's Day	Monday	Tuesday	Wednesday	Thursday	Friday	Saturday
27	☐ 14:22—15:23	☐ 16:1-22	☐ 17:1—18:8	☐ 18:9—19:21	☐ 20:1—21:17	☐ 21:18—22:30	☐ 23:1-25
28	☐ 24:1-22	☐ 25:1-19	☐ 26:1-19	☐ 27:1-26	☐ 28:1-68	☐ 29:1-29	☐ 30:1—31:29
29	☐ 31:30—32:52	☐ 33:1-29	☐ 34:1-12	☐ Josh 1:1-18	☐ 2:1-24	☐ 3:1-17	☐ 4:1-24
30	☐ 5:1-15	☐ 6:1-27	☐ 7:1-26	☐ 8:1-35	☐ 9:1-27	☐ 10:1-43	☐ 11:1—12:24
31	☐ 13:1-33	☐ 14:1—15:63	☐ 16:1—18:28	☐ 19:1-51	☐ 20:1—21:45	☐ 22:1-34	☐ 23:1—24:33
32	☐ Judg 1:1-36	☐ 2:1-23	☐ 3:1-31	☐ 4:1-24	☐ 5:1-31	☐ 6:1-40	☐ 7:1-25
33	☐ 8:1-35	☐ 9:1-57	☐ 10:1—11:40	☐ 12:1—13:25	☐ 14:1—15:20	☐ 16:1-31	☐ 17:1—18:31
34	☐ 19:1-30	☐ 20:1-48	☐ 21:1-25	☐ Ruth 1:1-22	☐ 2:1-23	☐ 3:1-18	☐ 4:1-22
35	☐ 1 Sam 1:1-28	☐ 2:1-36	☐ 3:1—4:22	☐ 5:1—6:21	☐ 7:1—8:22	☐ 9:1-27	☐ 10:1—11:15
36	☐ 12:1—13:23	☐ 14:1-52	☐ 15:1-35	☐ 16:1-23	☐ 17:1-58	☐ 18:1-30	☐ 19:1-24
37	☐ 20:1-42	☐ 21:1—22:23	☐ 23:1—24:22	☐ 25:1-44	☐ 26:1-25	☐ 27:1—28:25	☐ 29:1—30:31
38	☐ 31:1-13	☐ 2 Sam 1:1-27	☐ 2:1-32	☐ 3:1-39	☐ 4:1—5:25	☐ 6:1-23	☐ 7:1-29
39	☐ 8:1—9:13	☐ 10:1—11:27	☐ 12:1-31	☐ 13:1-39	☐ 14:1-33	☐ 15:1—16:23	☐ 17:1—18:33
40	☐ 19:1-43	☐ 20:1—21:22	☐ 22:1-51	☐ 23:1-39	☐ 24:1-25	☐ 1 Kings 1:1-19	☐ 1:20-53
41	☐ 2:1-46	☐ 3:1-28	☐ 4:1-34	☐ 5:1—6:38	☐ 7:1-22	☐ 7:23-51	☐ 8:1-36
42	☐ 8:37-66	☐ 9:1-28	☐ 10:1-29	☐ 11:1-43	☐ 12:1-33	☐ 13:1-34	☐ 14:1-31
43	☐ 15:1-34	☐ 16:1—17:24	☐ 18:1-46	☐ 19:1-21	☐ 20:1-43	☐ 21:1—22:53	☐ 2 Kings 1:1-18
44	☐ 2:1—3:27	☐ 4:1-44	☐ 5:1—6:33	☐ 7:1-20	☐ 8:1-29	☐ 9:1-37	☐ 10:1-36
45	☐ 11:1—12:21	☐ 13:1—14:29	☐ 15:1-38	☐ 16:1-20	☐ 17:1-41	☐ 18:1-37	☐ 19:1-37
46	☐ 20:1—21:26	☐ 22:1-20	☐ 23:1-37	☐ 24:1—25:30	☐ 1 Chron 1:1-54	☐ 2:1—3:24	☐ 4:1—5:26
47	☐ 6:1-81	☐ 7:1-40	☐ 8:1-40	☐ 9:1-44	☐ 10:1—11:47	☐ 12:1-40	☐ 13:1—14:17
48	☐ 15:1—16:43	☐ 17:1-27	☐ 18:1—19:19	☐ 20:1—21:30	☐ 22:1—23:32	☐ 24:1—25:31	☐ 26:1-32
49	☐ 27:1-34	☐ 28:1—29:30	☐ 2 Chron 1:1-17	☐ 2:1—3:17	☐ 4:1—5:14	☐ 6:1-42	☐ 7:1—8:18
50	☐ 9:1—10:19	☐ 11:1—12:16	☐ 13:1—15:19	☐ 16:1—17:19	☐ 18:1—19:11	☐ 20:1-37	☐ 21:1—22:12
51	☐ 23:1—24:27	☐ 25:1—26:23	☐ 27:1—28:27	☐ 29:1-36	☐ 30:1—31:21	☐ 32:1-33	☐ 33:1—34:33
52	☐ 35:1—36:23	☐ Ezra 1:1-11	☐ 2:1-70	☐ 3:1—4:24	☐ 5:1—6:22	☐ 7:1-28	☐ 8:1-36

Reading Schedule for the Recovery Version of the Old Testament with Footnotes

Wk.	Lord's Day	Monday	Tuesday	Wednesday	Thursday	Friday	Saturday
53	☐ 9:1—10:44	☐ Neh 1:1-11	☐ 2:1—3:32	☐ 4:1—5:19	☐ 6:1-19	☐ 7:1-73	☐ 8:1-18
54	☐ 9:1-20	☐ 9:21-38	☐ 10:1—11:36	☐ 12:1-47	☐ 13:1-31	☐ Esth 1:1-22	☐ 2:1—3:15
55	☐ 4:1—5:14	☐ 6:1—7:10	☐ 8:1-17	☐ 9:1—10:3	☐ Job 1:1-22	☐ 2:1—3:26	☐ 4:1—5:27
56	☐ 6:1—7:21	☐ 8:1—9:35	☐ 10:1—11:20	☐ 12:1—13:28	☐ 14:1—15:35	☐ 16:1—17:16	☐ 18:1—19:29
57	☐ 20:1—21:34	☐ 22:1—23:17	☐ 24:1—25:6	☐ 26:1—27:23	☐ 28:1—29:25	☐ 30:1—31:40	☐ 32:1—33:33
58	☐ 34:1—35:16	☐ 36:1-33	☐ 37:1-24	☐ 38:1-41	☐ 39:1-30	☐ 40:1-24	☐ 41:1-34
59	☐ 42:1-17	☐ Psa 1:1-6	☐ 2:1—3:8	☐ 4:1—6:10	☐ 7:1—8:9	☐ 9:1—10:18	☐ 11:1—15:5
60	☐ 16:1—17:15	☐ 18:1-50	☐ 19:1—21:13	☐ 22:1-31	☐ 23:1—24:10	☐ 25:1—27:14	☐ 28:1—30:12
61	☐ 31:1—32:11	☐ 33:1—34:22	☐ 35:1—36:12	☐ 37:1-40	☐ 38:1—39:13	☐ 40:1—41:13	☐ 42:1—43:5
62	☐ 44:1-26	☐ 45:1-17	☐ 46:1—48:14	☐ 49:1—50:23	☐ 51:1—52:9	☐ 53:1—55:23	☐ 56:1—58:11
63	☐ 59:1—61:8	☐ 62:1—64:10	☐ 65:1—67:7	☐ 68:1-35	☐ 69:1—70:5	☐ 71:1—72:20	☐ 73:1—74:23
64	☐ 75:1—77:20	☐ 78:1-72	☐ 79:1—81:16	☐ 82:1—84:12	☐ 85:1—87:7	☐ 88:1—89:52	☐ 90:1—91:16
65	☐ 92:1—94:23	☐ 95:1—97:12	☐ 98:1—101:8	☐ 102:1—103:22	☐ 104:1—105:45	☐ 106:1-48	☐ 107:1-43
66	☐ 108:1—109:31	☐ 110:1—112:10	☐ 113:1—115:18	☐ 116:1—118:29	☐ 119:1-32	☐ 119:33-72	☐ 119:73-120
67	☐ 119:121-176	☐ 120:1—124:8	☐ 125:1—128:6	☐ 129:1—132:18	☐ 133:1—135:21	☐ 136:1—138:8	☐ 139:1—140:13
68	☐ 141:1—144:15	☐ 145:1—147:20	☐ 148:1—150:6	☐ Prov 1:1-33	☐ 2:1—3:35	☐ 4:1—5:23	☐ 6:1-35
69	☐ 7:1—8:36	☐ 9:1—10:32	☐ 11:1—12:28	☐ 13:1—14:35	☐ 15:1-33	☐ 16:1-33	☐ 17:1-28
70	☐ 18:1-24	☐ 19:1—20:30	☐ 21:1—22:29	☐ 23:1-35	☐ 24:1—25:28	☐ 26:1—27:27	☐ 28:1—29:27
71	☐ 30:1-33	☐ 31:1-31	☐ Eccl 1:1-18	☐ 2:1—3:22	☐ 4:1—5:20	☐ 6:1—7:29	☐ 8:1—9:18
72	☐ 10:1—11:10	☐ 12:1-14	☐ S.S 1:1-8	☐ 1:9-17	☐ 2:1-17	☐ 3:1-11	☐ 4:1-8
73	☐ 4:9-16	☐ 5:1-16	☐ 6:1-13	☐ 7:1-13	☐ 8:1-14	☐ Isa 1:1-11	☐ 1:12-31
74	☐ 2:1-22	☐ 3:1-26	☐ 4:1-6	☐ 5:1-30	☐ 6:1-13	☐ 7:1-25	☐ 8:1-22
75	☐ 9:1-21	☐ 10:1-34	☐ 11:1—12:6	☐ 13:1-22	☐ 14:14	☐ 14:15-32	☐ 15:1—16:14
76	☐ 17:1—18:7	☐ 19:1-25	☐ 20:1—21:17	☐ 22:1-25	☐ 23:1-18	☐ 24:1-23	☐ 25:1-12
77	☐ 26:1-21	☐ 27:1-13	☐ 28:1-29	☐ 29:1-24	☐ 30:1-33	☐ 31:1—32:20	☐ 33:1-24
78	☐ 34:1-17	☐ 35:1-10	☐ 36:1-22	☐ 37:1-38	☐ 38:1—39:8	☐ 40:1-31	☐ 41:1-29

Reading Schedule for the Recovery Version of the Old Testament with Footnotes

Wk.	Lord's Day	Monday	Tuesday	Wednesday	Thursday	Friday	Saturday
79	42:1-25	43:1-28	44:1-28	45:1-25	46:1-13	47:1-15	48:1-22
80	49:1-13	49:14-26	50:1—51:23	52:1-15	53:1-12	54:1-17	55:1-13
81	56:1-12	57:1-21	58:1-14	59:1-21	60:1-22	61:1-11	62:1-12
82	63:1-19	64:1-12	65:1-25	66:1-24	Jer 1:1-19	2:1-19	2:20-37
83	3:1-25	4:1-31	5:1-31	6:1-30	7:1-34	8:1-22	9:1-26
84	10:1-25	11:1—12:17	13:1-27	14:1-22	15:1-21	16:1—17:27	18:1-23
85	19:1—20:18	21:1—22:30	23:1-40	24:1—25:38	26:1—27:22	28:1—29:32	30:1-24
86	31:1-23	31:24-40	32:1-44	33:1-26	34:1-22	35:1-19	36:1-32
87	37:1-21	38:1-28	39:1—40:16	41:1—42:22	43:1—44:30	45:1—46:28	47:1—48:16
88	48:17-47	49:1-22	49:23-39	50:1-27	50:28-46	51:1-27	51:28-64
89	52:1-34	Lam 1:1-22	2:1-22	3:1-39	3:40-66	4:1-22	5:1-22
90	Ezek 1:1-14	1:15-28	2:1—3:27	4:1—5:17	6:1—7:27	8:1—9:11	10:1—11:25
91	12:1—13:23	14:1—15:8	16:1-63	17:1—18:32	19:1-14	20:1-49	21:1-32
92	22:1-31	23:1-49	24:1-27	25:1—26:21	27:1-36	28:1-26	29:1—30:26
93	31:1—32:32	33:1-33	34:1-31	35:1—36:21	36:22-38	37:1-28	38:1—39:29
94	40:1-27	40:28-49	41:1-26	42:1—43:27	44:1-31	45:1-25	46:1-24
95	47:1-23	48:1-35	Dan 1:1-21	2:1-30	2:31-49	3:1-30	4:1-37
96	5:1-31	6:1-28	7:1-12	7:13-28	8:1-27	9:1-27	10:1-21
97	11:1-22	11:23-45	12:1-13	Hosea 1:1-11	2:1-23	3:1—4:19	5:1-15
98	6:1-11	7:1-16	8:1-14	9:1-17	10:1-15	11:1-12	12:1-14
99	13:1—14:9	Joel 1:1-20	2:1-16	2:17-32	3:1-21	Amos 1:1-15	2:1-16
100	3:1-15	4:1—5:27	6:1—7:17	8:1—9:15	Obad 1-21	Jonah 1:1-17	2:1—4:11
101	Micah 1:1-16	2:1—3:12	4:1—5:15	6:1—7:20	Nahum 1:1-15	2:1—3:19	Hab 1:1-17
102	2:1-20	3:1-19	Zeph 1:1-18	2:1-15	3:1-20	Hag 1:1-15	2:1-23
103	Zech 1:1-21	2:1-13	3:1-10	4:1-14	5:1—6:15	7:1—8:23	9:1-17
104	10:1—11:17	12:1—13:9	14:1-21	Mal 1:1-14	2:1-17	3:1-18	4:1-6

Reading Schedule for the Recovery Version of the New Testament with Footnotes

Wk.	Lord's Day	Monday	Tuesday	Wednesday	Thursday	Friday	Saturday
1	☐ Matt 1:1-2	☐ 1:3-7	☐ 1:8-17	☐ 1:18-25	☐ 2:1-23	☐ 3:1-6	☐ 3:7-17
2	☐ 4:1-11	☐ 4:12-25	☐ 5:1-4	☐ 5:5-12	☐ 5:13-20	☐ 5:21-26	☐ 5:27-48
3	☐ 6:1-8	☐ 6:9-18	☐ 6:19-34	☐ 7:1-12	☐ 7:13-29	☐ 8:1-13	☐ 8:14-22
4	☐ 8:23-34	☐ 9:1-13	☐ 9:14-17	☐ 9:18-34	☐ 9:35—10:5	☐ 10:6-25	☐ 10:26-42
5	☐ 11:1-15	☐ 11:16-30	☐ 12:1-14	☐ 12:15-32	☐ 12:33-42	☐ 12:43—13:2	☐ 13:3-12
6	☐ 13:13-30	☐ 13:31-43	☐ 13:44-58	☐ 14:1-13	☐ 14:14-21	☐ 14:22-36	☐ 15:1-20
7	☐ 15:21-31	☐ 15:32-39	☐ 16:1-12	☐ 16:13-20	☐ 16:21-28	☐ 17:1-13	☐ 17:14-27
8	☐ 18:1-14	☐ 18:15-22	☐ 18:23-35	☐ 19:1-15	☐ 19:16-30	☐ 20:1-16	☐ 20:17-34
9	☐ 21:1-11	☐ 21:12-22	☐ 21:23-32	☐ 21:33-46	☐ 22:1-22	☐ 22:23-33	☐ 22:34-46
10	☐ 23:1-12	☐ 23:13-39	☐ 24:1-14	☐ 24:15-31	☐ 24:32-51	☐ 25:1-13	☐ 25:14-30
11	☐ 25:31-46	☐ 26:1-16	☐ 26:17-35	☐ 26:36-46	☐ 26:47-64	☐ 26:65-75	☐ 27:1-26
12	☐ 27:27-44	☐ 27:45-56	☐ 27:57—28:15	☐ 28:16-20	☐ Mark 1:1	☐ 1:2-6	☐ 1:7-13
13	☐ 1:14-28	☐ 1:29-45	☐ 2:1-12	☐ 2:13-28	☐ 3:1-19	☐ 3:20-35	☐ 4:1-25
14	☐ 4:26-41	☐ 5:1-20	☐ 5:21-43	☐ 6:1-29	☐ 6:30-56	☐ 7:1-23	☐ 7:24-37
15	☐ 8:1-26	☐ 8:27—9:1	☐ 9:2-29	☐ 9:30-50	☐ 10:1-16	☐ 10:17-34	☐ 10:35-52
16	☐ 11:1-16	☐ 11:17-33	☐ 12:1-27	☐ 12:28-44	☐ 13:1-13	☐ 13:14-37	☐ 14:1-26
17	☐ 14:27-52	☐ 14:53-72	☐ 15:1-15	☐ 15:16-47	☐ 16:1-8	☐ 16:9-20	☐ Luke 1:1-4
18	☐ 1:5-25	☐ 1:26-46	☐ 1:47-56	☐ 1:57-80	☐ 2:1-8	☐ 2:9-20	☐ 2:21-39
19	☐ 2:40-52	☐ 3:1-20	☐ 3:21-38	☐ 4:1-13	☐ 4:14-30	☐ 4:31-44	☐ 5:1-26
20	☐ 5:27—6:16	☐ 6:17-38	☐ 6:39-49	☐ 7:1-17	☐ 7:18-23	☐ 7:24-35	☐ 7:36-50
21	☐ 8:1-15	☐ 8:16-25	☐ 8:26-39	☐ 8:40-56	☐ 9:1-17	☐ 9:18-26	☐ 9:27-36
22	☐ 9:37-50	☐ 9:51-62	☐ 10:1-11	☐ 10:12-24	☐ 10:25-37	☐ 10:38-42	☐ 11:1-13
23	☐ 11:14-26	☐ 11:27-36	☐ 11:37-54	☐ 12:1-12	☐ 12:13-21	☐ 12:22-34	☐ 12:35-48
24	☐ 12:49-59	☐ 13:1-9	☐ 13:10-17	☐ 13:18-30	☐ 13:31—14:6	☐ 14:7-14	☐ 14:15-24
25	☐ 14:25-35	☐ 15:1-10	☐ 15:11-21	☐ 15:22-32	☐ 16:1-13	☐ 16:14-22	☐ 16:23-31
26	☐ 17:1-19	☐ 17:20-37	☐ 18:1-14	☐ 18:15-30	☐ 18:31-43	☐ 19:1-10	☐ 19:11-27

Reading Schedule for the Recovery Version of the New Testament with Footnotes

Wk.	Lord's Day	Monday	Tuesday	Wednesday	Thursday	Friday	Saturday
27	☐ Luke 19:28-48	☐ 20:1-19	☐ 20:20-38	☐ 20:39—21:4	☐ 21:5-27	☐ 21:28-38	☐ 22:1-20
28	☐ 22:21-38	☐ 22:39-54	☐ 22:55-71	☐ 23:1-43	☐ 23:44-56	☐ 24:1-12	☐ 24:13-35
29	☐ 24:36-53	☐ John 1:1-13	☐ 1:14-18	☐ 1:19-34	☐ 1:35-51	☐ 2:1-11	☐ 2:12-22
30	☐ 2:23—3:13	☐ 3:14-21	☐ 3:22-36	☐ 4:1-14	☐ 4:15-26	☐ 4:27-42	☐ 4:43-54
31	☐ 5:1-16	☐ 5:17-30	☐ 5:31-47	☐ 6:1-15	☐ 6:16-31	☐ 6:32-51	☐ 6:52-71
32	☐ 7:1-9	☐ 7:10-24	☐ 7:25-36	☐ 7:37-52	☐ 7:53—8:11	☐ 8:12-27	☐ 8:28-44
33	☐ 8:45-59	☐ 9:1-13	☐ 9:14-34	☐ 9:35—10:9	☐ 10:10-30	☐ 10:31—11:4	☐ 11:5-22
34	☐ 11:23-40	☐ 11:41-57	☐ 12:1-11	☐ 12:12-24	☐ 12:25-36	☐ 12:37-50	☐ 13:1-11
35	☐ 13:12-30	☐ 13:31-38	☐ 14:1-6	☐ 14:7-20	☐ 14:21-31	☐ 15:1-11	☐ 15:12-27
36	☐ 16:1-15	☐ 16:16-33	☐ 17:1-5	☐ 17:6-13	☐ 17:14-24	☐ 17:25—18:11	☐ 18:12-27
37	☐ 18:28-40	☐ 19:1-16	☐ 19:17-30	☐ 19:31-42	☐ 20:1-13	☐ 20:14-18	☐ 20:19-22
38	☐ 20:23-31	☐ 21:1-14	☐ 21:15-22	☐ 21:23-25	☐ Acts 1:1-8	☐ 1:9-14	☐ 1:15-26
39	☐ 2:1-13	☐ 2:14-21	☐ 2:22-36	☐ 2:37-41	☐ 2:42-47	☐ 3:1-18	☐ 3:19—4:22
40	☐ 4:23-37	☐ 5:1-16	☐ 5:17-32	☐ 5:33-42	☐ 6:1—7:1	☐ 7:2-29	☐ 7:30-60
41	☐ 8:1-13	☐ 8:14-25	☐ 8:26-40	☐ 9:1-19	☐ 9:20-43	☐ 10:1-16	☐ 10:17-33
42	☐ 10:34-48	☐ 11:1-18	☐ 11:19-30	☐ 12:1-25	☐ 13:1-12	☐ 13:13-43	☐ 13:44—14:5
43	☐ 14:6-28	☐ 15:1-12	☐ 15:13-34	☐ 15:35—16:5	☐ 16:6-18	☐ 16:19-40	☐ 17:1-18
44	☐ 17:19-34	☐ 18:1-17	☐ 18:18-28	☐ 19:1-20	☐ 19:21-41	☐ 20:1-12	☐ 20:13-38
45	☐ 21:1-14	☐ 21:15-26	☐ 21:27-40	☐ 22:1-21	☐ 22:22-29	☐ 22:30—23:11	☐ 23:12-15
46	☐ 23:16-30	☐ 23:31—24:21	☐ 24:22—25:5	☐ 25:6-27	☐ 26:1-13	☐ 26:14-32	☐ 27:1-26
47	☐ 27:27—28:10	☐ 28:11-22	☐ 28:23-31	☐ Rom 1:1-2	☐ 1:3-7	☐ 1:8-17	☐ 1:18-25
48	☐ 1:26—2:10	☐ 2:11-29	☐ 3:1-20	☐ 3:21-31	☐ 4:1-12	☐ 4:13-25	☐ 5:1-11
49	☐ 5:12-17	☐ 5:18—6:5	☐ 6:6-11	☐ 6:12-23	☐ 7:1-12	☐ 7:13-25	☐ 8:1-2
50	☐ 8:3-6	☐ 8:7-13	☐ 8:14-25	☐ 8:26-39	☐ 9:1-18	☐ 9:19—10:3	☐ 10:4-15
51	☐ 10:16—11:10	☐ 11:11-22	☐ 11:23-36	☐ 12:1-3	☐ 12:4-21	☐ 13:1-14	☐ 14:1-12
52	☐ 14:13-23	☐ 15:1-13	☐ 15:14-33	☐ 16:1-5	☐ 16:6-24	☐ 16:25-27	☐ 1 Cor 1:1-4

Reading Schedule for the Recovery Version of the New Testament with Footnotes

Wk.	Lord's Day	Monday	Tuesday	Wednesday	Thursday	Friday	Saturday
53	☐ 1 Cor 1:5-9	☐ 1:10-17	☐ 1:18-31	☐ 2:1-5	☐ 2:6-10	☐ 2:11-16	☐ 3:1-9
54	☐ 3:10-13	☐ 3:14-23	☐ 4:1-9	☐ 4:10-21	☐ 5:1-13	☐ 6:1-11	☐ 6:12-20
55	☐ 7:1-16	☐ 7:17-24	☐ 7:25-40	☐ 8:1-13	☐ 9:1-15	☐ 9:16-27	☐ 10:1-4
56	☐ 10:5-13	☐ 10:14-33	☐ 11:1-6	☐ 11:7-16	☐ 11:17-26	☐ 11:27-34	☐ 12:1-11
57	☐ 12:12-22	☐ 12:23-31	☐ 13:1-13	☐ 14:1-12	☐ 14:13-25	☐ 14:26-33	☐ 14:34-40
58	☐ 15:1-19	☐ 15:20-28	☐ 15:29-34	☐ 15:35-49	☐ 15:50-58	☐ 16:1-9	☐ 16:10-24
59	☐ 2 Cor 1:1-4	☐ 1:5-14	☐ 1:15-22	☐ 1:23—2:11	☐ 2:12-17	☐ 3:1-6	☐ 3:7-11
60	☐ 3:12-18	☐ 4:1-6	☐ 4:7-12	☐ 4:13-18	☐ 5:1-8	☐ 5:9-15	☐ 5:16-21
61	☐ 6:1-13	☐ 6:14—7:4	☐ 7:5-16	☐ 8:1-15	☐ 8:16-24	☐ 9:1-15	☐ 10:1-6
62	☐ 10:7-18	☐ 11:1-15	☐ 11:16-33	☐ 12:1-10	☐ 12:11-21	☐ 13:1-10	☐ 13:11-14
63	☐ Gal 1:1-5	☐ 1:6-14	☐ 1:15-24	☐ 2:1-13	☐ 2:14-21	☐ 3:1-4	☐ 3:5-14
64	☐ 3:15-22	☐ 3:23-29	☐ 4:1-7	☐ 4:8-20	☐ 4:21-31	☐ 5:1-12	☐ 5:13-21
65	☐ 5:22-26	☐ 6:1-10	☐ 6:11-15	☐ 6:16-18	☐ Eph 1:1-3	☐ 1:4-6	☐ 1:7-10
66	☐ 1:11-14	☐ 1:15-18	☐ 1:19-23	☐ 2:1-5	☐ 2:6-10	☐ 2:11-14	☐ 2:15-18
67	☐ 2:19-22	☐ 3:1-7	☐ 3:8-13	☐ 3:14-18	☐ 3:19-21	☐ 4:1-4	☐ 4:5-10
68	☐ 4:11-16	☐ 4:17-24	☐ 4:25-32	☐ 5:1-10	☐ 5:11-21	☐ 5:22-26	☐ 5:27-33
69	☐ 6:1-9	☐ 6:10-14	☐ 6:15-18	☐ 6:19-24	☐ Phil 1:1-7	☐ 1:8-18	☐ 1:19-26
70	☐ 1:27—2:4	☐ 2:5-11	☐ 2:12-16	☐ 2:17-30	☐ 3:1-6	☐ 3:7-11	☐ 3:12-16
71	☐ 3:17-21	☐ 4:1-9	☐ 4:10-23	☐ Col 1:1-8	☐ 1:9-13	☐ 1:14-23	☐ 1:24-29
72	☐ 2:1-7	☐ 2:8-15	☐ 2:16-23	☐ 3:1-4	☐ 3:5-15	☐ 3:16-25	☐ 4:1-18
73	☐ 1 Thes 1:1-3	☐ 1:4-10	☐ 2:1-12	☐ 2:13—3:5	☐ 3:6-13	☐ 4:1-10	☐ 4:11—5:11
74	☐ 5:12-28	☐ 2 Thes 1:1-12	☐ 2:1-17	☐ 3:1-18	☐ 1 Tim 1:1-2	☐ 1:3-4	☐ 1:5-14
75	☐ 1:15-20	☐ 2:1-7	☐ 2:8-15	☐ 3:1-13	☐ 3:14—4:5	☐ 4:6-16	☐ 5:1-25
76	☐ 6:1-10	☐ 6:11-21	☐ 2 Tim 1:1-10	☐ 1:11-18	☐ 2:1-15	☐ 2:16-26	☐ 3:1-13
77	☐ 3:14—4:8	☐ 4:9-22	☐ Titus 1:1-4	☐ 1:5-16	☐ 2:1-15	☐ 3:1-8	☐ 3:9-15
78	☐ Philem 1:1-11	☐ 1:12-25	☐ Heb 1:1-2	☐ 1:3-5	☐ 1:6-14	☐ 2:1-9	☐ 2:10-18

Reading Schedule for the Recovery Version of the New Testament with Footnotes

Wk.	Lord's Day	Monday	Tuesday	Wednesday	Thursday	Friday	Saturday
79	Heb 3:1-6	3:7-19	4:1-9	4:10-13	4:14-16	5:1-10	5:11—6:3
80	6:4-8	6:9-20	7:1-10	7:11-28	8:1-6	8:7-13	9:1-4
81	9:5-14	9:15-28	10:1-18	10:19-28	10:29-39	11:1-6	11:7-19
82	11:20-31	11:32-40	12:1-2	12:3-13	12:14-17	12:18-26	12:27-29
83	13:1-7	13:8-12	13:13-15	13:16-25	James 1:1-8	1:9-18	1:19-27
84	2:1-13	2:14-26	3:1-18	4:1-10	4:11-17	5:1-12	5:13-20
85	1 Pet 1:1-2	1:3-4	1:5	1:6-9	1:10-12	1:13-17	1:18-25
86	2:1-3	2:4-8	2:9-17	2:18-25	3:1-13	3:14-22	4:1-6
87	4:7-16	4:17-19	5:1-4	5:5-9	5:10-14	2 Pet 1:1-2	1:3-4
88	1:5-8	1:9-11	1:12-18	1:19-21	2:1-3	2:4-11	2:12-22
89	3:1-6	3:7-9	3:10-12	3:13-15	3:16	3:17-18	1 John 1:1-2
90	1:3-4	1:5	1:6	1:7	1:8-10	2:1-2	2:3-11
91	2:12-14	2:15-19	2:20-23	2:24-27	2:28-29	3:1-5	3:6-10
92	3:11-18	3:19-24	4:1-6	4:7-11	4:12-15	4:16—5:3	5:4-13
93	5:14-17	5:18-21	2 John 1:1-3	1:4-9	1:10-13	3 John 1:1-6	1:7-14
94	Jude 1:1-4	1:5-10	1:11-19	1:20-25	Rev 1:1-3	1:4-6	1:7-11
95	1:12-13	1:14-16	1:17-20	2:1-6	2:7	2:8-9	2:10-11
96	2:12-14	2:15-17	2:18-23	2:24-29	3:1-3	3:4-6	3:7-9
97	3:10-13	3:14-18	3:19-22	4:1-5	4:6-7	4:8-11	5:1-6
98	5:7-14	6:1-8	6:9-17	7:1-8	7:9-17	8:1-6	8:7-12
99	8:13—9:11	9:12-21	10:1-4	10:5-11	11:1-4	11:5-14	11:15-19
100	12:1-4	12:5-9	12:10-18	13:1-10	13:11-18	14:1-5	14:6-12
101	14:13-20	15:1-8	16:1-12	16:13-21	17:1-6	17:7-18	18:1-8
102	18:9—19:4	19:5-10	19:11-16	19:17-21	20:1-6	20:7-10	20:11-15
103	21:1	21:2	21:3-8	21:9-13	21:14-18	21:19-21	21:22-27
104	22:1	22:2	22:3-11	22:12-15	22:16-17	22:18-21	

Week 1 — Day 6   Today's verses

1 Pet. So then let those also who suffer accord-
4:19   ing to the will of God commit their souls
      in well-doing to a faithful Creator.
2:24 Who Himself bore up our sins in His body
      on the tree, in order that we, having died
      to sins, might live to righteousness; by
      whose bruise you were healed.

_____
       Date

Week 1 — Day 5   Today's verses

1 Pet. ...All of you gird yourselves with humility
5:5-6 toward one another, because God resists
      the proud but gives grace to the humble.
      Therefore be humbled under the mighty
      hand of God that He may exalt you in due
      time.

_____
       Date

Week 1 — Day 4   Today's verses

1 Pet. ...Christ also suffered on your behalf...;
2:21-24 who committed no sin, nor was guile
      found in His mouth; who being reviled
      did not revile in return; suffering, He did
      not threaten but kept committing *all* to
      Him who judges righteously; who Him-
      self bore up our sins in His body on the
      tree, in order that we, having died to sins,
      might live to righteousness; by whose
      bruise you were healed.

_____
       Date

Week 1 — Day 3   Today's verses

1 Pet. Beloved, do not think that the fiery ordeal
4:12-13 among you, coming to you for a trial, is
      strange...but inasmuch as you share in
      the sufferings of Christ, rejoice, so that
      also at the revelation of His glory you may
      rejoice exultingly.
2:21 For to this you were called, because
      Christ also suffered on your behalf, leav-
      ing you a model so that you may follow in
      His steps.

_____
       Date

Week 1 — Day 2   Today's verses

1 Pet. But according to the Holy One who
1:15-17 called you, you yourselves also be holy in
      all *your* manner of life; because it is writ-
      ten, "You shall be holy because I am
      holy." And if you call as Father the One
      who without respect of persons judges
      according to each one's work, pass the
      time of your sojourning in fear.

_____
       Date

Week 1 — Day 1   Today's verses

1 Pet. For it is time for the judgment to begin
4:17   from the house of God; and if first from us,
      what will be the end of those who disobey
      the gospel of God?

_____
       Date

Week 2 — Day 4   Today's verses

1 Pet. Be sober; watch. Your adversary, the
5:8-9 devil, as a roaring lion, walks about, seeking someone to devour. Him withstand, being firm in your faith, knowing that the same sufferings are being accomplished among your brotherhood in the world.

2 Pet. Expecting and hastening the coming of
3:12-13 the day of God, on account of which the heavens, being on fire, will be dissolved, and the elements, burning with intense heat, are to be melted away. But according to His promise we are expecting new heavens and a new earth, in which righteousness dwells.

_____
Date

Week 2 — Day 5   Today's verses

1 Pet. Let your adorning not be the out-
3:3-4 ward....but the hidden man of the heart in the incorruptible *adornment* of a meek and quiet spirit, which is very costly in the sight of God.

4:14 If you are reproached in the name of Christ, you are blessed, because the Spirit of glory and of God rests upon you.

1:11 Searching into what *time* or what manner of time the Spirit of Christ in them was making clear, testifying beforehand of the sufferings of Christ and the glories after these.

_____
Date

Week 2 — Day 6   Today's verses

2 Pet. And count the long-suffering of our Lord
3:15-16 *to be* salvation, even as also our beloved brother Paul, according to the wisdom given to him, wrote to you, as also in all *his* letters, speaking in them concerning these things, in which some things are hard to understand, which the unlearned and unstable twist, as also the rest of the Scriptures, to their own destruction.

_____
Date

Week 2 — Day 1   Today's verses

1 Pet. Chosen according to the foreknowledge
1:2 of God the Father in the sanctification of the Spirit unto the obedience and sprinkling of the blood of Jesus Christ...

2:24 Who Himself bore up our sins in His body on the tree, in order that we, having died to sins, might live to righteousness; by whose bruise you were healed.

3:18 For Christ also has suffered once for sins, the Righteous on behalf of the unrighteous, that He might bring you to God, on the one hand being put to death in the flesh, but on the other, made alive in the Spirit.

_____
Date

Week 2 — Day 2   Today's verses

2 Pet. Seeing that His divine power has granted
1:3-4 to us all things which relate to life and godliness, through the full knowledge of Him who has called us by His own glory and virtue, through which He has granted to us precious and exceedingly great promises that through these you might become partakers of the divine nature, having escaped the corruption which is in the world by lust.

1 Pet. But the God of all grace, He who has
5:10 called you into His eternal glory in Christ Jesus, after you have suffered a little while, will Himself perfect, establish, strengthen, *and ground you.*

_____
Date

Week 2 — Day 3   Today's verses

1 Pet. Blessed be the God and Father of our Lord
1:3-5 Jesus Christ, who according to His great mercy has regenerated us unto a living hope through the resurrection of Jesus Christ from the dead, unto an inheritance, incorruptible and undefiled and unfading, kept in the heavens for you, who are being guarded by the power of God through faith unto a salvation ready to be revealed at the last time.

2 Pet. For in this way the entrance into the eter-
1:11 nal kingdom of our Lord and Savior Jesus Christ will be richly *and* bountifully supplied to you.

_____
Date

Week 3 — Day 4   Today's verses

1 Pet. Blessed be the God and Father of our Lord
1:3-4 Jesus Christ, who...has regenerated us unto a living hope through the resurrection of Jesus Christ from the dead, unto an inheritance, incorruptible and undefiled and unfading, kept in the heavens for you.

10-11 Concerning this salvation the prophets, who prophesied concerning the grace *that was to come* unto you, sought and searched diligently, searching into what *time* or what manner of time the Spirit of Christ in them was making clear, testifying beforehand of the sufferings of Christ and the glories after these.

Heb. ...Christ, who through the eternal Spirit of-
9:14 fered Himself without blemish to God...

Date _____

Week 3 — Day 5   Today's verses

1 Pet. But according to the Holy One who
1:15-16 called you, you yourselves also be holy in all *your* manner of life; because it is written, "You shall be holy because I am holy."

Eph. Blessed be the God and Father of our Lord
1:3 Jesus Christ, who has blessed us with every spiritual blessing in the heavenlies in Christ.

Date _____

Week 3 — Day 6   Today's verses

1 Pet. For this is grace, if anyone, because of a
2:19 consciousness of God, bears sorrows by suffering unjustly.

Rom. For God is my witness, whom I serve in
1:9 my spirit in the gospel of His Son, how unceasingly I make mention of you always in my prayers.

2 Pet. Grace to you and peace be multiplied in
1:2 the full knowledge of God and of Jesus our Lord.

3:18 But grow in the grace and knowledge of our Lord and Savior Jesus Christ. To Him be the glory both now and unto the day of eternity. Amen.

Date _____

Week 3 — Day 1   Today's verses

1 Pet. Peter, an apostle of Jesus Christ, to the so-
1:1-2 journers of the dispersion,...chosen according to the foreknowledge of God the Father in the sanctification of the Spirit unto the obedience and sprinkling of the blood of Jesus Christ: Grace to you and peace be multiplied.

20 Who was foreknown before the foundation of the world but has been manifested in the last of times for your sake.

Date _____

Week 3 — Day 2   Today's verses

1 Pet. Chosen according to the foreknowledge
1:2 of God the Father in the sanctification of the Spirit unto the obedience and sprinkling of the blood of Jesus Christ...

Eph. Even as He chose us in Him before the
1:4 foundation of the world to be holy and without blemish before Him in love.

John And when I [the Comforter] comes, He
16:8 will convict the world concerning sin and concerning righteousness and concerning judgment.

Date _____

Week 3 — Day 3   Today's verses

1 Pet. Blessed be the God and Father of our Lord
1:3 Jesus Christ, who according to His great mercy has regenerated us unto a living hope through the resurrection of Jesus Christ from the dead.

18-19 Knowing that *it was* not with corruptible things, with silver or gold, *that* you were redeemed from your vain manner of life handed down from your fathers, but with precious blood, as of a Lamb without blemish and without spot, *the blood* of Christ.

23 Having been regenerated not of corruptible seed but of incorruptible, through *the* living and abiding word of God.

Date _____

Week 4 — Day 1   **Today's verses**

1 Pet. 1:3 Blessed be the God and Father of our Lord Jesus Christ, who according to His great mercy has regenerated us unto a living hope through the resurrection of Jesus Christ from the dead.

1 Pet. 1:5 Who are being guarded by the power of God through faith unto a salvation ready to be revealed at the last time.

John 3:16 For God so loved the world that He gave His only begotten Son, that everyone who believes into Him would not perish, but would have eternal life.

Date _____

Week 4 — Day 2   **Today's verses**

Rom. 6:22 But now, having been freed from sin and enslaved to God, you have your fruit unto sanctification, and the end, eternal life.

Rom. 8:2 For the law of the Spirit of life has freed me in Christ Jesus from the law of sin and of death.

Rom. 12:2 And do not be fashioned according to this age, but be transformed by the renewing of the mind that you may prove what the will of God is, that which is good and well pleasing and perfect.

Date _____

Week 4 — Day 3   **Today's verses**

Rom. 8:23 ...We ourselves,...who have the firstfruits of the Spirit, even we ourselves groan in ourselves, eagerly awaiting sonship, the redemption of our body.

Phil. 3:21 Who will transfigure the body of our humiliation to be conformed to the body of His glory, according to His operation by which He is able even to subject all things to Himself.

1 Thes. 2:12 So that you might walk in a manner worthy of God, who calls you into His own kingdom and glory.

Date _____

Week 4 — Day 4   **Today's verses**

1 Pet. 1:9 Receiving the end of your faith, the salvation of your souls.

1 Pet. 1:13 Therefore girding up the loins of your mind *and* being sober, set your hope perfectly on the grace being brought to you at the revelation of Jesus Christ.

John 12:25 He who loves his soul-life loses it; and he who hates his soul-life in this world shall keep it unto eternal life.

Date _____

Week 4 — Day 5   **Today's verses**

Matt. 16:25 ...Whoever wants to save his soul-life shall lose it; but whoever loses his soul-life for My sake shall find it.

Matt. 25:21 His master said to him, Well *done*, good and faithful slave. You were faithful over a few things; I will set you over many things. Enter into the joy of your master.

2 Pet. 1:11 For in this way the entrance into the eternal kingdom of our Lord and Savior Jesus Christ will be richly *and* bountifully supplied to you.

Date _____

Week 4 — Day 6   **Today's verses**

Luke 9:24-25 For whoever wants to save his soul-life shall lose it; but whoever loses his soul-life for My sake, this one shall save it. For what is a man profited if he gains the whole world but loses or forfeits himself?

Heb. 10:39 But we are not of those who shrink back to ruin but of them who have faith to the gaining of the soul.

Date _____

Week 5 — Day 1

Today's verses

Matt. 13:3 ...He spoke many things to them in parables, saying, Behold, the sower went out to sow.

1 Cor. 3:6-7, 9 I planted, Apollos watered, but God caused the growth. So then neither is he who plants anything nor he who waters, but God who causes the growth....For we are God's fellow workers; you are God's cultivated land, God's building.

1 Pet. 2:4-5 Coming to Him, a living stone, rejected by men but with God chosen *and* precious, you yourselves also, as living stones, are being built up as a spiritual house into a holy priesthood to offer up spiritual sacrifices acceptable to God through Jesus Christ.

_____
Date

Week 5 — Day 2

Today's verses

1 Pet. 2:5 You yourselves also, as living stones, are being built up as a spiritual house...

John 1:42 He led him to Jesus. Looking at him, Jesus said, You are Simon, the son of John; you shall be called Cephas (which is interpreted, Peter).

Matt. 16:16-18 ...Peter answered and said, You are the Christ, the Son of the living God. And Jesus answered and said to him, Blessed are you, Simon Barjona, because flesh and blood has not revealed *this* to you, but My Father who is in the heavens. And I also say to you that you are Peter, and upon this rock I will build My church, and the gates of Hades shall not prevail against it.

_____
Date

Week 5 — Day 3

Today's verses

Eph. 2:21 In whom all the building, being fitted together, is growing into a holy temple in the Lord.

Psa. 139:23-24 Search me, O God, and know my heart; try me, and know my anxious thoughts; and see if there is some harmful way in me, and lead me on the eternal way.

_____
Date

Week 5 — Day 4

Today's verses

1 Cor. 2:14-15 ...A soulish man does not receive the things of the Spirit of God, for they are foolishness to him and he is not able to know *them* because they are discerned spiritually. But the spiritual man discerns all things, but he himself is discerned by no one.

_____
Date

Week 5 — Day 5

Today's verses

1 Pet. 2:1-3 Therefore putting away all malice and all guile and hypocrisies and envyings and all evil speakings, as newborn babes, long for the guileless milk of the word in order that by it you may grow unto salvation, if you have tasted that the Lord is good.

_____
Date

Week 5 — Day 6

Today's verses

1 Pet. 2:5 You yourselves also, as living stones, are being built up as a spiritual house into a holy priesthood to offer up spiritual sacrifices acceptable to God through Jesus Christ.

9 But you are a chosen race, a royal priesthood, a holy nation, a people acquired for a possession, so that you may tell out the virtues of Him who has called you out of darkness into His marvelous light.

_____
Date

Week 6 — Day 4

Today's verses

Gal. 4:19 My children, with whom I travail again in birth until Christ is formed in you.

Eph. 3:16-17 That He would grant you, according to the riches of His glory, to be strengthened with power through His Spirit into the inner man, that Christ may make His home in your hearts through faith...

Date

Week 6 — Day 5

Today's verses

1 Pet. 1:15 But according to the Holy One who called you, you yourselves also be holy in all *your* manner of life.

2:12 Having your manner of life excellent among the Gentiles, so that in the matter concerning which they speak against you as evildoers they may, by your good works, as they see *them* with their own eyes, glorify God in the day of *His* visitation.

3:16 ...Having a good conscience, so that in the matter in which you are spoken against, those who revile your good manner of life in Christ may be put to shame.

Date

Week 6 — Day 6

Today's verses

1 Pet. 1:2 Chosen according to the foreknowledge of God the Father in the sanctification of the Spirit unto the obedience and sprinkling of the blood of Jesus Christ: Grace to you and peace be multiplied.

16 Because it is written, "You shall be holy because I am holy."

Heb. 12:10 For they disciplined for a few days as it seemed good to them; but He, for what is profitable that we might partake of His holiness.

Date

Week 6 — Day 1

Today's verses

1 Pet. 2:20-23 ...But if, while doing good and suffering, you endure, this is grace with God. For to this you were called, because Christ also suffered on your behalf, leaving you a model so that you may follow in His steps; who committed no sin, nor was guile found in His mouth; who being reviled did not revile in return; suffering, He did not threaten but kept committing *all* to Him who judges righteously.

Date

Week 6 — Day 2

Today's verses

Matt. 11:28-29 Come to Me all who toil and are burdened, and I will give you rest. Take My yoke upon you and learn from Me, for I am meek and lowly in heart, and you will find rest for your souls.

Rom. 8:29 Because those whom He foreknew, He also predestinated *to be* conformed to the image of His Son, that He might be the Firstborn among many brothers.

Date

Week 6 — Day 3

Today's verses

Gal. 2:20 I am crucified with Christ; and *it is* no longer I *who* live, but *it is* Christ *who* lives in me; and the *life* which I now live in the flesh I live in faith, the *faith* of the Son of God, who loved me and gave Himself up for me.

John 14:19 Yet a little while and the world beholds Me no longer, but you behold Me; because I live, you also shall live.

Phil. 1:21 For to me, to live is Christ...

Date